THE LIFE OF PADRE PIO

GENNARO PREZIUSO

THE LIFE OF PADRE PIO

Between the Altar and the Confessional

Translated and Edited by
JORDAN AUMANN, OP

ST PAULS

Originally published in Italian by Edizioni San Paolo, s.r.l.,
under the title *Padre Pio: apostolo del confessionale.*

Library of Congress Cataloging-in-Publication Data

Preziuso, Gennaro.
   [Padre Pio. English]
   The life of Padre Pio: between the altar and the confessional
/ Gennaro Preziuso; translated and edited by Jordan Aumann.
     p.   cm.
   Includes bibliographical references.
   ISBN 0-8189-0831-9
   1. Pio, padre, 1887-1968. 2. Capuchins — Italy Biography.
  3. Stigmatics — Italy Biography. 4. Catholic Church — Italy —
Clergy   Biography. 5. Christian saints — Italy Biography. I. Aumann,
Jordan.   II. Title.
   BX4700.P7755P74   2000
   271'.3602 — dc21   99-40385
   [B]   CIP

Produced and designed in the United States of America by the
Fathers and Brothers of the Society of St. Paul,
2187 Victory Boulevard, Staten Island, New York 10314-6603,
as part of their communications apostolate.

ISBN: 978-0-8189-0831-6

Printing Information:

Current Printing - first digit   5 6 7 8 9 10

Year of Current Printing - first year shown

              2017 2018 2019 2020 2021 2022

CONTENTS

PREFACE

$\mathcal{T}$HE PRESENT BIOGRAPHY FOCUSES EX-
clusively on Blessed Padre Pio of Pietrelcina, an extraordinary
man of God who has made Jesus Crucified visible to us in our
day by becoming a humanly perfect image of him.

I have tried to speak about him by letting him speak as
much as possible, and he does this through his letters, which
constitute a monumental collection under the title *Epistolario*.
Normally I give exact references to his letters when I quote
his words, but in order to avoid weighing the text down with
numerous notes, I have not given precise references for quota-
tions from his confreres, his spiritual sons and daughters, and
those who were close to him during his many years at San
Giovanni Rotondo. They were all drawn to him by a mysterious attraction and then completely captivated by his virtues,
his humanity, and his mode of living the Christian life and
making its influence felt.

Padre Pio has taught and still teaches us how to forgive,
how to practice fraternal charity, to be silent when we cannot
praise, to avoid criticism that divides and separates, that feeds
discord and contention, thus disturbing souls and consciences.
Consequently, out of respect for his example and teaching, I have
tried to preserve an air of peace and serenity by distancing
myself from polemics and negative criticism.

I have reserved special space for anything that the Sovereign Pontiffs have said of him, and especially Pope John Paul II, because his words have long anticipated the positive judgment of the Church.

I hope that this work will help to make Padre Pio better known and will stimulate a sincere admiration and devotion that will lead to imitation.

THE LIFE OF PADRE PIO

1

PIETRELCINA

$\mathscr{S}$ET IN THE MIDST OF AN ENCHANTING panorama and surrounded by the barren hills of Sannio, some twelve kilometers (7.5 miles) from Benevento, Pietrelcina greets the eye of the visitor spread out on a rocky projection some 350 meters or 1200 feet above sea level. The history of its origin is uncertain, except that someone, after discovering archeological evidence containing an inscription with a dedication to Jove, wanted to trace it back to Roman times, presuming that there had once been a pagan temple there. But history is silent in that respect. The medieval chronicler in the year 1100 speaks of a baronial castle built "on huge, hard rocks and surrounded by a wall with two doors, one on the north and the other on the south, with a huge inaccessible rock on the east."

The etymology of the name which, according to legend, has undergone changes in the course of centuries, is also uncertain. According to civic and parish documents, it was first called *Pietra,* and then *Pietra Pulcina* or *Pietra Pucina* to distinguish it from Pietra Maiore, which rose near the Tammaro River in the field of San Giorgio La Molara.

On the other hand, according to another ancient legend, the name *Pietra* was changed to *Pietra Elcina*, in honor of the fairy Elginia, who dwelt in the area; or to *Pietra Porcina*, after the killing of a wild boar that took place in a cave adjacent to the castle; or to

Pietrapucina, when in the excavation of the parish church a stone slab was found on which had been carved a hen with her chicks (*pulcini*); or finally, to *Pietrelcina*, referring to an evergreen oak (*elce*) that was found growing among the rocks and stones. Ultimately it was that evergreen oak, with a serpent wrapped around its trunk, that became the civic coat of arms for that region.

In 1138 the baronial castle was attacked and burned by the Norman, William Ruggero II. The castle was restored in 1173 by William II but it was razed to the ground in the catastrophic earthquake of 1373. It was again rebuilt by the renowned jurist Bartolomeo Camerario of Benevento.

Around the feudal fortress, which was definitively destroyed by another earthquake in 1688, had risen a cluster of houses, one leaning against another, and all of them huddled within the rocky mass called "Morgia." The old quarter was given the name "Rione Castello" and is readily accessible from the piazza, after one has passed through the Porto Madonella and traversed a series of narrow, winding streets.

Today the town is inhabited by simple working people who are friendly and respectful, bound to tradition and given primarily to work in the fields. The Forgione family has lived in this region since 1881. Grazio Maria Forgione was born on October 23, 1860. Cheerful, young, intelligent and of short stature, he would rise early in the morning. Then he would saddle his donkey, wrap a piece of bread in a large handkerchief, make sure that there was a flask of wine and a piece of cheese in the saddle bag, and start out on the path that leads to Piana Romana. He was considered a landowner because in the rural district he had a bit of property for farming, a little less than a hectare (2.5 acres) of land, and he also had a rustic lean-to measuring about 30 square meters (98 sq. yds.). The floor was paved with stones, the roof was supported by heavy timbers, and the walls were made of unfinished stone. It was very useful for storing hay and for spending the night during harvest time.

Grazio worked all day long, fertilizing and pruning the olive trees and planting or harvesting wheat or corn. In the evening he liked to be in good company. He was often recruited to serenade the girls of the area. He would sing ecstatically the most beautiful love songs while his friends accompanied his singing with guitar and mandolins. Being an energetic and adventurous youth, he would flirt with one girl after another until he met Maria Giuseppa Di Nunzio.

Giuseppa was a typical domestic type from Castello. Slender and amiable, she was an ordinary girl but she had the makings of a great lady. She had a handsome dowry and she could have waited for a much better match if she had not fallen in love with Grazio and decided to marry him.

In the summertime she usually dressed in a white blouse with a skirt that reached to her ankles. On her head she always wore a freshly laundered kerchief. During the winter she threw a shawl around her shoulders. She was always very cordial and respectful towards everyone. In the early mornings she went several times to the water fountain, carrying a large jug on her head to provide the water supply for the day. She was very good at kneading dough for bread and then taking it to the district oven for baking. She was very religious. In addition to Fridays, she abstained from meat on Wednesdays in honor of Our Lady of Mount Carmel and on Saturdays in honor of the Our Lady of the Rosary of Pompeii. She attended church at St. Mary of the Angels, which contained the miraculous statue of the *Madonna della Libera* or at the old parish church of Santa Anna which housed the relics of the martyr San Pio.

Grazio and Giuseppa were married on June 8, 1881, and they moved in with Giuseppa's family on Via Santa Maria degli Angeli. When their first child, Michele, was born on June 25, 1882, they moved to Vico Storto Valle. There they lived in a building in which the rooms were separated at some distance from one another. For example, the bedroom was at No. 27, the kitchen was several meters down the street, and there was another room at the top of a steep staircase which, because of its location, was called the tower room. Giuseppa kept busy in these rooms from morning until night, except when her help was needed in the fields alongside her husband.

After Michele, there were two other children: Francesco, born on February 12, 1884, and Amalia, born on May 20, 1885. But these two little angels soon flew back to heaven, Francesco on March 3, 1884, and Amalia on February 14, 1887. When Amalia died, Giuseppa was already pregnant with her fourth child. She prayed fervently to the Lord for the infant she was carrying in her womb and anxiously awaited the joyful event.

2

EARLY CHILDHOOD

*G*IUSEPPA WAS GETTING READY TO PUT the last tools under cover on the farm when she experienced a sharp pain. Others followed and they became more and more frequent. She leaned against the wall and pressed her lips together in silence. She recognized the labor pains that preceded delivery and immediately removed her apron. She should have stayed at home, but there was so much to do on the farm and she had wanted to give Grazio a hand on that day.

Being a woman of strong temperament, she concealed her pain in order not to alarm her husband. With a thin voice she simply said: "Grazio, I'm going... I don't feel well." Then she started out on the mule-track that leads to Pietrelcina and disappeared amid the thick vegetation. All of a sudden she felt as if the child was going to be born then and there. Panting, she stopped on the wooden bridge and mentally commended herself to St. Anne, the patroness of women in labor. Then she resumed her homeward journey. Exhausted, she finally reached home and with the help of the midwife, Grazia Formichelli, she gave birth to a boy, the future Padre Pio.

The rough stones of Rione Castello, bathed in light, dozed in the lukewarm peace of twilight. The chimneys of the ancient houses were smoking as the women were busy preparing supper.

The wind whistled through the winding streets of town making whirlwinds on the pavement. In the valley, the torrent of the Pantaniello River ran merrily along, singing a new song.

It was May 25, 1887. The clock in the church tower pointed to five o'clock in the afternoon.

About an hour later, trotting along on the back of his donkey, Grazio arrived at the house. Neighbors along the street broke the good news and offered congratulations. With difficulty he made his way through the door to the bedroom, which was filled with people. He embraced his wife, gave her a flower, and then with a surge of pride and with great joy in his heart, he held aloft their newborn son, who immediately let his voice be heard.

Then the midwife said: "I want to inform you that the baby was born wrapped in a white veil. It is a good sign. He will surely be great and prosperous."

Mamma Peppa (as Giuseppa was called by her friends and neighbors) simply added: "As God wills!" She had wanted the baby to be baptized on the very day of his birth. If this took place, according to popular belief, a soul would be liberated from Purgatory. But it was already too late in the day.

The following morning Grazio went to the municipal building to inscribe his son in the birth registry. The written document is still preserved in the communal archives with the number 77 and it reads as follows.

> In the year one thousand eight hundred and eighty-seven, on the twenty-sixth day of May, at the hour of nine and some minutes before noon... in the Municipal Building.
>
> Before me, *Gaetano Sagliocca* ... Acting Mayor and Official of the Civil State of Pietrelcina, has appeared *Grazio Forgione, son of Michele,* twenty-six years of age, with residence in Pietrelcina, who has declared to me that at the hour of five in the afternoon, in the house located in Vico Storto Valle, number twenty-five, of *Maria Giuseppa Di Nunzio,* his wife, twenty-eight years of age...

was born an infant of the masculine sex, to whom he is giving the name *Francesco*...

Witnesses to the foregoing and to this registration are here present: *Luciano di Giuseppe Pennisi*, thirty-nine years of age, shoemaker, and *Antonio Orlando, son of Michele*, forty-two years of age, landowner, both of whom are residents of this township.

Immediately afterwards Grazio went to the neighboring parish church to have the infant baptized. The sacrament of baptism was administered by Father Nicolantonio in the presence of Grazia Formichelli, who acted as godmother. In the register of baptisms the priest wrote that Francesco was born at the 22nd hour of the day (10:00 p.m.) instead of at the 17th hour (5:00 p.m.). However, the disagreement is only apparent, because both numbers refer to the same time. The difference lies in the manner in which the time was computed. The priest was using a medieval method, which made the curfew at the 19th hour (7:00 p.m.) equivalent to the end of the day at midnight (24:00), and the baby was born two hours before curfew.

Francesco was a very beautiful baby. The neighbors competed with one another to hold him. But during the night he was the despair of all who were near him because he cried constantly. On one occasion when his father was trying to go to sleep and get some rest, he became so annoyed that he lost his patience and jumped out of bed, saying: "Is it possible that a devil has been born into this house instead of a Christian!"

That sent a shudder through Mamma Peppa. Taking the infant in her arms, she asked with disapproval: "What do you want me to do with the creature?" An argument ensued.

The incident was described in later years by Padre Pio himself, who added: "From that night on, I didn't cry anymore." Then he explained: "I cried out of fear. As soon as my mother put out the light, all kinds of monsters approached me and they disappeared only when the light was turned on again. It was the devil tormenting me!"

After some months the Forgione family, like most other parents in Pietrelcina, took Francesco to a fortune-teller named Giuseppe Fajella in Porta Madonnella. At the conclusion of the ceremony, Fajella pronounced a mysterious prophecy: "This baby will be honored throughout the world. Through his hands will pass vast amounts of money, but he will own none of it. He will suffer much and one day everyone will want to touch him without being able to do so."

Grazio and Peppa returned home crestfallen. They thought about that prophecy for a long time and finally concluded: "Maybe when he is grown up, Francesco will go to America and make a fortune, but he will not be able to invest his money."

In Pietrelcina the people mingled with their religious practices the popular folklore in which fortune-tellers and healers played an important and sometimes decisive role. In fact, in addition to Fajella, who studied the stars and worked out horoscopes, there were others who made use of methods akin to magic and claimed to be able to cure certain ailments, to get rid of the evil eye (*malocchio*) and to produce permanent healings.

Mamma Peppa also had recourse to one of these means when Francesco was two years old and suffered severe abdominal pains. She made the sign of the cross over the baby's stomach and began reciting a series of prayers and incantations, and very soon the little one got on his feet and was running around.

Padre Pio recounted this story later on and then added with a smile: "Poor me! That lady picked me up as you would a little lamb."

The Forgione couple had three daughters later on: Felicita, September 15, 1889; Pellegrina, March 15, 1892; and Grazia, December 27, 1894. The family lived in a peaceful atmosphere of work, love, and the fear of God. In the morning, Mamma Peppe would dress and feed the children in a hurry and then give them to the care of their grandmother or neighbors. Then she would join Grazio in the fields to watch over the cow, the goats or the pigs or else to water her flowers at the edge of their plot of land.

In the early afternoon she would return home with a basket of fruit and vegetables and busy herself preparing the evening supper. She poured the corn flour into the pan to make a first serving of polenta. Then she fried a bit of pasta, kept in the kneading trough, which the children liked very much. If there were no cheese or sausage, she would make breaded cakes of ricotta.

When the hoof-beats of the donkey on the pavement announced the arrival of Grazio, the little ones all ran to greet their father, who would take out of his jacket some fruit such as pears or a melon. With a smile of approval, Mamma Peppa would set the table and, after giving thanks to God, would enjoy seeing how the family devoured the food she had prepared. The same ritual was repeated every day with only slight variations.

After supper in the summertime, the family went to church for the evening service. In the winter, on the other hand, they sat in a semicircle around the fireplace, and Mamma Peppa would reach into the pocket of her apron, take out her beads and slowly begin the holy rosary. Grazio and the children responded together to the prayers until the eyes of the smallest ones began to close and their heads began to nod like bells moved by the wind.

The only one who was not overcome by sleep was Francesco. He kept his gaze fixed on the log burning in the fireplace and he realized that in his little heart something began to be inflamed: a love larger than himself. The mysteries of the rosary, which Mamma Peppa narrated like so many chapters in a long, enchanting story, attracted and captivated him more and more.

Giuseppa confided to a friend that as he grew up through the years, "Francesco never committed any fault; he was never unruly; he was a good boy and always obedient. Every morning and every evening he went to visit Jesus and the Madonna. He never went out with the other boys to cause trouble; rather, he stayed away from them."

If occasionally he was corrected, it was only for some small thing in dealing with his sisters. He didn't care to go out and play with children his own age because, as he said, "They are not honest, they use bad language, and they swear." One day he heard a blasphemous expression and he went home crying. For that reason, he preferred to remain by himself or to go to church with his grandmother.

3

CAUGHT UP
IN HEAVENLY THINGS

$\mathscr{W}$E KNOW FROM THE TESTIMONY OF FRA Luca of Pietrelcina that "Francesco loved to draw apart from everyone and be recollected in prayer. If the oratory was closed, he would remain in prayer seated on a rock until his mother called him." He would return again as soon as possible and be admitted to the church by the sacristan Peruto who, at the hour agreed upon, would open the church door to let him out.

One morning, all alone in the pews, he was listening to the crackling noise of the sanctuary lamp which stood before the tabernacle. After a while, Jesus appeared and made a sign for him to approach, and when he did, Jesus laid his hand upon his head. That gesture signified a choice, a call to which Francesco, only five years old at the time, generously responded, formulating the intention to consecrate himself entirely to God. From that moment on, his thoughts were fixed constantly on heavenly things.

But Satan was lying in wait. A confirmation of how he manifested himself is found in the *Diary* of one of his spiritual directors, Padre Agostino de San Marco, who made the following entry in 1915:

> The ecstasies and apparitions began when he was five years old and had the thought and desire to consecrate

himself forever to the Lord. At the time supernatural interventions were practically continuous. When asked why he had concealed this for such a long time, he answered candidly that he did not speak of it because he thought this was ordinary and it happened to all souls. In fact, one morning he asked ingenuously: "And you, don't you see the Madonna?" On hearing the negative response, he retorted: "You only say that out of holy humility!"

The diabolical apparitions also began when he was five years old, and for almost twenty years he was tormented by obscene images in human form or in the form of ferocious animals.

Francesco habitually frequented the parish church and soon he began to serve Mass. Every Sunday he was always the first one to arrive for the catechism lesson in the early afternoon. He was eager to learn the principles of Catholic doctrine and to know the lives of the saints so that he could imitate their example. One afternoon, in fact, he went out dressed in a new garment that his parents had just bought for him. A few hours later he returned home half naked. His response to his mother's scolding was: "I gave it to a little boy who needed it more than I did."

Mamma Peppa was amazed at this, and on the following day she discreetly and cautiously followed her little son, because she suspected that there was something extraordinary about him. He also surprised his mother by frequently sleeping on the floor instead of his comfortable bed, using a stone for a pillow.

Once she heard strange noises coming from the room next to the kitchen. She entered and found Francesco taking the discipline with an iron chain. Astounded and worried, she demanded an explanation and he replied: "Mamma, I must strike myself like Jesus was struck!" On another occasion some neighbor boys told her that her son was hitting himself with a hemp rope. With her head in her hands, Giuseppa wept.

At the age of ten, Francesco began to prepare himself with extreme care for his First Communion. In the following year, when Francesco saw that the parish priest, Father Giovanni Caporaso, had arranged for decorating the altar with many beautiful white flowers in preparation for the ceremony, his joy knew no bounds.

Nothing else seemed to interest him; he liked only to celebrate the religious feasts. With his hand in the hand of his father, he would march in the various processions in honor of the Madonna, wearing a necklace of chestnuts. He was thrilled with everything: the processional statues, the music, the lights, the bonfires, the offering of first-fruits to the Virgin Mary and — why not? — the piece of nougat candy (*torrone*) that he shared with his brother and sisters on his return home.

At Christmas time he lived in a magical world, filled with wonderful images. In the evenings during the Christmas novena he followed the bag-pipers who stopped inside or in front of the houses with the sacred images which were then placed at the intersection of the streets. He would get up early in the morning and go to church with his mother to attend Mass and sing a hymn to the Infant Jesus. At home there was a rectangular niche carved into the wall. There, Francesco arranged his Christmas crib (*presepe*). With the help of a friend named Luigino, he carved out of clay the figures of the shepherds, the Madonna, St. Joseph and the Infant Jesus. This last statue, as one of his childhood friends, Mercurio Scocca, recalls, involved a great deal of work because "he made it and then made it all over again several times." He was never satisfied with the result, and he said: "It didn't turn out as I wanted!" For lights, thanks to a lucky find, they put a few drops of olive oil and a wick in a snail's shell. They would go out into the field to find the most beautiful snail shell, but Luigino would have to dig out the snail because Francesco did not like to perform the "operation."

One particular event had a special attraction for Francesco. It was the pilgrimage which proceeded from Pietrelcina and terminated in Benevento, Bari or Montevergine. One time Grazio agreed to take Francesco to the shrine of St. Pellegrino, martyr, in the province of Avellino. Francesco did not close his eyes all the night before. In the morning he sat on the donkey in front of his father and to be sure he would not fall off, he was fastened to the saddle with a rope. The trip lasted several hours, and when they arrived, they gave the donkey shelter at the local tavern and then made their way to the church. There was such a crowd of people that it was only with difficulty that they made their way close to the altar dedicated to St. Pellegrino.

After reciting the prayers, Grazio took his son by the hand to start the trip back home, but Francesco begged him to wait a while. The boy was rooted to the spot, looking at a scene that greatly affected him. A mother held in her arms a deformed baby which was more a mass of flesh than a recognizable infant. Weeping, she was praying to St. Pellegrino for the poor creature. Francesco identified completely with the woman's sorrow and he joined his prayers to hers.

Suddenly the mother, weeping and exhausted, placed the baby on the altar and cried out: "San Pellegrino, if you don't want to heal him, it's better that you take him back!"

In an instant the baby stood up on his own two feet, completely cured, and toddled forward saying, "Mamma!"

The people cried out excitedly at the miracle and fell on their knees in prayer around the altar. The ringing of the church bell announced the cure. Francesco, amazed at what had happened, was unable to move because of the crush of the crowd. That was the first of a series of marvelous events that would punctuate his life.

The tenth year of Francesco's life was marked by another remarkable happening. Because of a serious intestinal disorder, he was confined to his bed for more than a month. During that time he was fed only spoonfuls of milk, which he swallowed with great difficulty and only to please his mother.

Giuseppa did not know how she could divide her time between caring for her son and the harvest, which also called for her help in the fields.

One day she fried a large batch of sweet peppers in olive oil. She put aside half of it in the sideboard and the other half she took to the men who were working in the field with her husband. On leaving the house, she told Francesco to be a good boy and that she would be back soon.

In the meantime, the room was filled with the aroma of the fried peppers, which awakened the appetite of the sick boy. Standing on a chair, he took the plate filled with fried peppers, which were still warm, and in his great hunger, he avidly ate practically all of them. He went back to bed and fell asleep.

When his mother returned, she found him with his face redder than the *pepperoni*, confused and bathed in perspiration. Fearing that her child may have mistakenly taken a dose of the wrong medicine, she hastened to call the doctor. He came at once and after looking at the child's tongue, he took his temperature. Francesco did not have a fever, although he was in a very listless state. The doctor gave orders to suspend all medication and not to start any new treatments. He promised to return the following day. During the night the *pepperoni* produced a stupendous reaction and the child's intestines were freed of their blockage. The next day Francesco was able to get out of bed.

On September 27, 1899, Bishop Donato Maria Dell'Olio of Benevento administered the sacrament of confirmation in the parish church of Pietrelcina. Francesco, having completed twelve years, was among the twenty-two children to be confirmed. That event remained sculpted in his memory. Fifteen years later, while staying at Pietrelcina, in a letter to Padre Agostino, he recalled the feelings he had on that occasion:

> During these past few days we have had a visit from Archbishop Bonazzi, who is here to confer confirmation... I wept because of the consolation I felt in my heart as a result of this sacred ceremony. It called to mind what the Holy Paraclete made me feel on the day that I received the sacrament of confirmation, a very special day and unforgettable for the rest of my life.

How many sweet emotions this consoling Spirit made me feel on that day! When I think of it, I feel completely ignited by that living flame which burns and consumes but causes no pain (*Epistolario*, I, 471).

Francesco was big for his age, a little man, and Grazio would sometimes take Francesco with him and his older brother Michele out to the fields. There he assigned four sheep and a goat to his care and showed him how to pasture the animals.

The little shepherd was happy to have received a chore. Now he could spend much time admiring the beauty of nature, which he loved. In the silence he could hear much more clearly the voice of God, who with his Holy Spirit was fashioning Francesco's soul and drawing him to himself.

On the threshing-floor Francesco met Fra Camillo, a Capuchin from the neighboring town of Morcone. He was on a trip begging for alms and had stopped at the Forgione farm. He had a rosy face and a long beard that gave him an austere appearance.

Mamma Peppa was generous to him and she filled his knapsack. Fra Camillo thanked her, gave a friendly pat and a medal to the little shepherd, and then disappeared among the trees.

The image of the Capuchin mendicant from Morcone, his deportment and his long beard, made a strong impression on Francesco who frequently recalled their meeting.

In the meantime Francesco had made friends with two other little shepherds, Mercurio Scocca and Ubaldo Vecchiarino. After eating his lunch, Francesco would take up the cross made out of two pieces of wood and march in procession. The others did not always take part. Mercurio would rather play, and he would protest: "That's enough! Always processions! Always processions!"

On one occasion Uncle Pellegrino called his nephew and said to him: "Franni, you have fast legs; take this money and buy me a Tuscan cigar and a box of matches."

The boy immediately set out on the errand. On the way home, he stopped on the bridge across the Pantaniello River and he was unable to resist the temptation. Imitating the gestures of his uncle, he lit the cigar and at the first puff he became dizzy and had an upset stomach. When he recovered, he returned to the farm and told his uncle everything that had happened. His uncle exploded in a fit of laughter. That was the first and last time that Francesco had anything to do with smoking.

In the evening, together with his companions, he used to go to the home of Mennato Saginario, an educated farmer who taught Francesco how to read for less than a *lira* a month. Then, during the day, while the sheep were grazing, Francesco would open his book and, running his index finger under the line, he would review the lesson.

Seeing his son study, Grazio said to himself: "Look, this son of mine is missing school, to take care of a few sheep!" Then talking it over with Giuseppa, the two of them decided that since Francesco had repeatedly expressed a desire to be enrolled in a regular course of studies, they would have him go to a private tutor.

First they sent him to Cosimo Scocca, and then to Domenico Tizzani, a man who had left the priesthood to marry and in order to support his wife and daughter was giving private lessons for five *lire* a month.

That amount of money, plus the expense for books, weighed heavily on the family budget. Grazio, however, did not lose heart. Since his work in Pietrelcina did not pay enough to cover expenses, he decided to emigrate to America so that his son could get an education.

4

"I WANT TO BE A MONK"

$\mathcal{A}$T THE AGE OF FIFTEEN, THE FUTURE
Padre Pio experienced his first ecstasy. He testified to this some
twenty years later in an autobiographical description of how
at that time the Lord was working in him.

> Ever since my birth, Jesus has shown me signs of
> special love. He has demonstrated that not only was he
> my Savior, my greatest Benefactor, but also my devoted,
> sincere and faithful Friend: a loving Friend, infinite love,
> my consolation, my joy, my comfort, my treasure.
>
> And, alas, innocently and unconsciously, I gave my
> heart, always burning with love for the All and for all,
> to created things that I found so pleasing and precious.
> He constantly watches over me; he took me back and
> reprimanded me interiorly, sweetly and paternally to be
> sure, but the scolding was felt in my soul.
>
> A sad but very sweet voice echoed in my poor
> heart; it was the instruction of a loving father pointing
> out to his son the dangers that he would encounter in
> life's struggles; the voice of a kind father who wants
> the heart of his son to be detached from those innocent,
> infantile loves; it was the voice of a loving father who
> whispered into the ear and the heart of his son to draw

him out of the clay and mire and jealously consecrate him entirely to himself.

Ardently, with loving sighs, with indescribable groans, with sweet and tender words, he called him to himself; he wanted to make him entirely his own... It seemed that he smiled at me; he seemed to be inviting me to another life; he made me understand that the secure gateway, the peaceful refuge for me was in the ranks of the ecclesiastical militia (*Epistolario,* III, 1006s).

Francesco remembered the figure of the Capuchin, Fra Camillo, and he asked Jesus:

"Where can I best serve you, Lord, if not in the cloister and under the banner of the Poverello of Assisi?" And, seeing my quandary, he smiled; he smiled for a long time; and such a smile left in my heart an ineffable sweetness, and I actually felt him so close to me that I seemed to see his shadow, and my flesh and my entire being exulted in my Savior, in my God... Within I heard a voice which insistently said to me: "Sanctify yourself and others" (*Epistolario,* III, 1010).

His vocation was now firmly planted in the heart of the shepherd of Pietrelcina. After assisting at Mass, meditating, praying, and fixing his gaze intently on Christ Crucified, he decided. Then, returning from school one day, he said to his mother: "Mamma, I want to become a monk. Yes, a monk who celebrates Mass. A monk with a beard."

His mother replied: "You are still a little boy. What do you know about having or not having a beard?"

Francesco then revealed his aspiration to the new parish priest, Salvatore Pannullo, who was affectionately called Don Tore. This priest had a great deal of experience in dealing with the question of vocations, since he had spent most of his priestly life at the Giannone School in Benevento. He understood the seriousness of the boy's desire and he consulted with Mamma Peppa and the uncle, Pellegrino. But Francesco also informed his father about his intention to consecrate himself entirely to God. Then he applied himself even more assiduously to his studies.

After he completed three years of schooling, his teacher Domenico Tizzani spoke with Mamma Peppa: "The boy is no longer getting anything out of his studies; nothing. He is always in the church; in the morning at Mass and in the afternoon at services. How can he learn anything?"

Francesco's mother reprimanded him and asked him to remember that in order to send him to school, his father had to emigrate to America. The boy listened in silence and then, weeping, he said: "Mamma, I am not the one who is not getting anything out of study, and it is not the Church that prevents me from learning; he is the one, he is a bad priest."

Mamma Peppa understood and she said nothing further.

When Grazio learned that his son wanted to become a monk, he said: "What more can a fallen-away priest teach him?" He then wrote to his wife, saying: "Take Francesco out of Tizzani's school at once and send him to a better one."

In a short time Giuseppa found a new teacher. His name was Angelo Càccavo who for thirty years had taught in the public schools of Pietrelcina and Cerreto. He willingly accepted Francesco and soon the boy began the program of studies for the secondary school and was first in the class. He would sit at his desk for hours, bent over his books. Vincenzo Salomone, a companion, said:

> I would go and call him: "Franci, do you want to play a game of *bottoni*?" He would look up and smile and give a sign meaning "Later, later!" I would return later and he would again give me the same sign, but always with a smile. I would go back so many times, until it was dark.

To reassure his father, Francesco wrote a letter to him on October 5, 1901, in which he said: "Now that I find myself under the guidance of a new teacher, I see that I am making progress from day to day, for which we are very content, both Mamma and myself."

His companions were envious of Francesco's high grades and they decided to play a mean trick on him. They convinced a girl in the class to write a love letter, which they secretly slipped into his pocket. Then, with repeated coughing, they caught the attention of the teacher.

"What's the matter?" he asked the students.

"Teacher, Francesco's in love," they replied.

While Francesco protested his innocence, his classmates pointed to his pocket. The teacher searched the boy and found the letter filled with passionate statements. The heavens opened!

"And you think you ought to become a monk!" he exclaimed. "Imagine that!" And the teacher slapped him and boxed his ears. Meanwhile, Francesco, weeping, kept repeating: "I don't know anything about that!"

The next day the girl who had written the letter was very remorseful and repentant, so she confessed everything to the teacher. He listened and then without saying anything, he gave her a kick.

Meanwhile, the family spoke of nothing but Francesco's vocation. Uncle Pellegrino had the parish priest Don Salvatore go to the friars to ask whether or not his nephew could enter the monastery. Accordingly, Don Salvatore wrote a letter to the Minister Provincial of the Capuchins, who replied: "There is no room in the novitiate at Morcone. He will have to wait."

Pellegrino suggested to his nephew that he should apply to the community of monks at Montevergine, who wear a white habit, a hat, shoes and are doing very well. But Francesco refused because they don't wear a beard.

Pellegrino then suggested they write to the Redemptorists at Sant'Angelo a Cupolo or to the Franciscans at Benevento. The nephew asked immediately; "But do they wear a beard?"

"No," answered Pellegrino.

Then Francesco's reply was also "No." No one could make him change his mind, because, as he said later as a priest, "the beard of Fra Camillo was fixed in my mind."

A few months passed and then the letter arrived from the Provincial of the Capuchins, giving Francesco a date on which he could enter. The parish priest, Don Salvatore took care of all the documents necessary for Francesco to enter the Capuchin novitiate at Morcone.

But the devil, hoping to block Francesco's passage into the monastery, launched a second attack. The parish priest received an anonymous letter stating that Francesco, the altar boy soon to become a friar, was courting the daughter of the station-master of Pietrelcina.

Don Salvatore experienced the bitterness of having been deceived. He sent for Francesco, and without giving him any explanation, he deprived him of any participation in religious functions and forbade him to wear the cassock and surplice.

Francesco was very much surprised, but he figured that it was the procedure to be followed before entering the monastery. Meanwhile, the parish priest arranged for Francesco to be spied upon in order to get at the truth of the matter. He also arranged for a handwriting expert to discover the author of the anonymous letter. It turned out that the culpable person was an altar boy companion who was jealous of Francesco and wanted to put him in a bad light because Francesco was more favored by the parish priest than himself.

Don Salvatore immediately explained to Francesco why he had removed him from service as an altar boy, and then he reinstated him. Moreover, Don Salvatore promised that as a recompense he would handle all the documentation for his entrance into the monastery free of charge.

Francesco hastened to the church to give thanks to the Madonna who, for the second time, had freed him from the calumnious accusations of his companions. But he bore no resentment against any of them; rather, he prayed for his accusers.

But Satan lost no time in presenting to Francesco's eyes "the sweet but false pleasures of this world with all their seductive attraction." The boy was aware of a desire to respond to the call of God and at the same time to the fascination of life and its pleasures. He spent sleepless nights, torn between opposite feelings. Then the Lord intervened with a vision. At his side appeared "a majestic man of great beauty, shining like the sun," who took him by the hand and said: "Come with me, because you are to fight as a valiant warrior." A little later, they were in an open field, in the middle of two groups drawn up on either side. One group was made up of "men with beautiful faces, dressed in white garments, as white as snow," but on the other side were "men of horrid appearance, dressed in black like dark phantoms." Francesco saw coming towards him a man of gigantic height whose forehead touched the clouds. His face was black and horrible.

The majestic "man of rare beauty" invited the boy to fight against the dreadful warrior. Francesco hesitated, but he heard a voice say: "All your resistance is in vain; with this one you must come to blows. Take courage; enter the struggle with confidence; advance courageously and I shall be with you; I shall assist you and I shall not let him conquer."

The fight took place, and with the help of the majestic man, the boy, spurred on by the applause of those dressed in white, won the victory over the ugly warrior, who fled cursing, together with the multitude of dark phantoms. The majestic man placed a crown on Francesco's head and as he departed, he said:

> I am reserving another crown more beautiful if you know how to struggle against the one with whom you have just fought. He will always return, always on the attack... Fight him valiantly and never doubt my assistance... Do not be frightened by his molestation and do not be afraid of his formidable appearance... I shall always be at your side, I shall always help you, so that you will always be victorious.

This vision, with its clearly defined details, gave the aspiring Capuchin novice a glimpse of his future: a constant struggle against the powers of hell (*Epistolario,* I, 1280s).

5

THE NOVITIATE

$\mathscr{F}$AR FROM THE TOWN, AT THE FOOT OF the mountain, surrounded by thick green vegetation, stands the austere monastery of the Capuchins of Morcone. The novitiate for "the friars with beards" was established in 1603. It contained about twenty small rooms which were ideal for the aspirants to the religious life during the year of probation, when they lived the full rigor of the Franciscan rule. This was the year of "novitiate" during which the candidates were expected to prove the authenticity of their vocation to the life of a Capuchin.

There was a small church, dedicated to Saints Philip and James, annexed to the monastery. Into this church, on January 6, 1903, came Francesco Forgione, accompanied by the young priest, Nicola Caruso, representing the pastor; the teacher, Angelo Càccavo; and two young friends, Vincenzo Masone and Antonio Bonavita.

After venerating Jesus in the Blessed Sacrament and the Madonna, Francesco was drawn to the little crib. While he gazed at the crib, for the benefit of his companions he pointed with his index finger at the statues of the Magi who had "arrived at the manger only a few hours ago." It was, in fact, the feast of Epiphany, a day which remained firmly impressed on the mind of Francesco, who would say years later to a spiritual daughter: "Today is the feast of Epiphany. On that day I left home."

The small group left the church and made their way to the monastery door, which was blackened with age. Don Nicola pulled on the cord of a little bell, which immediately made their presence known. Francesco was in the front of the group. For a moment there was dead silence but soon the scraping of sandals was heard. In the open doorway stood a Capuchin friar. It was Fra Camillo, the lay brother who had first aroused in little Francesco the desire to be "a monk with a beard."

The friar recognized Francesco immediately. He embraced him tightly and hugging him with fatherly affection, he said: "Eh! Franci! *Bravo!* You have been faithful to your promise and to the call of St. Francis." He then ushered them into the parlor and went off to notify the superior, Padre Francesco, and the master of novices, Padre Tommaso. The two Capuchins greeted the visitors warmly. After the introductions and the welcomes, it was time for the examination.

Francesco Forgione and Vincenzo Mansone were questioned on general culture, Italian, Latin, history and geography. They were interrogated by the commissary general of the Capuchin province, Padre Pio, and by the novice master. At the end of the examination the two boys were declared worthy of admission.

Then it was Antonio Bonavita's turn. He was also approved but because he had not yet reached the age stipulated by the Constitutions for admission to the novitiate, he had to return to Pietrelcina, to the dismay of the teacher Càccovo and the regret of Francesco and Vincenzo, who had hoped they could all enter the novitiate together.

Francesco and Vincenzo were then taken to the kitchen for some refreshments and then they had the afternoon free for visiting the monastery. Francesco returned for a moment to read what was written in large letters on the wall of the entrance: "Either penance or hell." Francesco did not hesitate in mentally making his choice. All his life had been directed to that penance to which Jesus in his preaching of the Kingdom of God had called all men and in particular to the penance practiced by the Seraphic Father, St. Francis of Assisi. Now Francesco's life, consecrated to God, would be a life of penance, but at that moment he promised that he would accept with joy every sort of mortification for the salvation of his own soul and the good of his neighbor. Anything but hell!

He intended to rejoin Vincenzo in order to share with him his intention and to urge him to make the same choice, but he came upon another plaque with the words "*Silentium, quia locus novitiorum est!*" that he translated: "Silence, for this is the place of the novitiate!" In order to preserve the interior spirit, to foster prayer, to study, to meditate, to hear the voice of God, silence would be the norm.

Francesco went back upstairs. On the landing his gaze fell on an ancient tapestry with a representation of the Sorrowful Mother, her eyes wet with tears. Underneath there was another Latin inscription: "*Hinc transire cave — nisi prius dixerit Ave*" (Take care not to pass here unless first you have said an Ave).

Francesco greeted the Madonna by giving her a kiss at the end of his index finger. Then he walked across the corridor. He glanced at the cells and was surprised that they were so small. Vincenzo was waiting for him, so together they went out into the garden and sat under a cypress tree to exchange their first impressions. From inside the monastery they could hear the voices of the friars who were chanting Vespers. It was winter, so very soon the shades of night would fall.

After supper, the master of novices took them to the cells assigned to them. Francesco's cell was No. 28 and on the wall was another inscription: "You are dead; and your life is hidden with Christ in God."

The young novice felt a shudder of fear, but then he entered the cell. Standing there all alone, in the middle of the four walls, he looked around. The furnishings consisted of a cot, a small table, a chair and a wash basin resting on a slender, somewhat rickety metal tripod. When all the lights were extinguished, a ray of moonlight illuminated the painful expression on the large crucifix hanging on one of the walls.

It was then that Francesco was seized with feelings of nostalgia. The image of his father came to mind, now far away across the ocean in America. He saw once again his home, his brother and sisters, his mother and relatives. His farewell to Mamma Peppa had been especially painful. He felt once again her arms around his neck and heard her voice: "My son, my heart is crushed; but don't think of your mother's sorrow. St. Francis is calling you and you must go."

At that moment the boy did not pray. Instead, he threw himself on his cot and burst into tears while the lump in his throat gradually dissolved. His lips kept pronouncing the one word: "Mamma." He kissed the rosary that he was holding in his hands. His mother had given it to him at the last moment as he was leaving. Soon drowsiness overtook him, so he curled up, pulled the covers around his shoulders, and dozed off. The next morning, the water in the clay pitcher was frozen, but Francesco broke the crust of ice, washed in the basin and then, filled with the love of God, started his new life in that oasis of peace.

Francesco learned the Franciscan way of life very quickly. He immediately memorized all he was taught about how to comport himself with his superiors and confreres. He also had to learn how to remain in bed after his examination of conscience and his prayers: to lie on his back, immobile, with his arms folded across his chest, because any movement would cause a rustling of the dry leaves in the mattress. He was to wear his own clothing for fifteen days, before his "vestition."

Finally the prophetic day arrived, the twenty-second day of that unforgettable month of January, 1903. Together with the other novices, he went into the monastery church. The entire community was gathered around the altar. The master of novices opened the solemn ceremony for the vestition of the aspirants to the religious life in the Capuchin habit. Each gesture was accompanied by a prayer formula of great significance: "May the Lord strip you of the old man... and vest you in the garb of the new man who according to God is created in justice and in the holiness of truth." Then Francesco, assisted by the acolytes, took off his civilian clothes and, after kissing it, put on the Capuchin tunic made of very coarse material.

Then, while Francesco was putting on the cowl, the master payed: "O Lord, put the hood of salvation on his head that he may overcome the snares of the devil." Next, as the novice placed the white cord around his waist, the master prayed: "May the Lord gird you with the cincture of purity and extinguish in your loins the heat of lust so that the virtues of continence and chastity may remain in you."

Finally, Francesco was given a lighted candle which he held before him so that the flame gave his countenance a crystalline appearance. Fra Tommaso then read the final prayer: "Receive the light of Christ as a symbol of your immortality, so that dead to the world, you may live in God. Rise from the dead. Christ will illumine you!"

When the *Veni Creator Spiritus* (Come, Holy Spirit) was intoned, Francesco could not hold back his tears. He was so deeply moved! He no longer belonged to the world. And to symbolize his complete surrender, he even changed his name. From that moment on he would no longer be known as Francesco Forgione, but Fra Pio of Pietrelcina. The new name was given to him by the superior, possibly to honor the minister provincial, Padre Pio of Benevento.

That day was a feast day in the monastery. Everyone was happy, but Fra Pio experienced the greatest joy when he read the document composed by the master of novices:

> J.M.J.F. — Morcone, January 22, 1903. The cleric, Fra Pio of Pietrelcina, known in the world as Francesco Forgione, with the permission of Very Reverend Pio of Benevento and under the decree of the Most Reverend Father General, dated January 21, 1903, was vested in the habit of probation by me, Fra Tommaso of Monte Sant'Angelo, master of novices, on this day January 22, 1903 at nine o'clock in the morning, in this our church

at Morcone, before the main altar in the presence of the professed religious and novices.

At last, he had officially entered religious life.

Fra Pio began his new life with extraordinary fervor, practicing extreme austerity, exhausting rigor, firm discipline and constant mortification. Those religious "didn't play games," and especially not Padre Tommaso, who was a religious through and through, a very good religious, understanding, but very severe.

He arranged for the fledgling friars a week of reflection in which the novices, after understanding what it means to be a real Capuchin, will have the opportunity to converse only with the Lord. For some, the perpetual silence was unbearable, but for Fra Pio it provided the opportunity to spend the time in profound recollection and intimate union with God.

Fra Giangiuseppe, an older novice who had been assigned as special companion for Fra Pio, scrupulously explained to him all the details regarding the observances. In the evening, before going to bed, the assigned prayers were recited, followed by the examination of conscience. Then, the novice would stretch out on the mattress, still wearing his religious habit. In this position, prescribed as a form of mortification, he should wear on the right side of his chest a large crucifix attached to a cord. At every stirring of temptation, he was supposed to kiss the crucifix repeatedly.

In the middle of the night the wooden clapper would signal the time to start the chanting of Matins of the Divine Office. The friars would immediately assemble in the choir to praise the Lord together, "following the example of the royal Psalmist, the saints and the ancient fathers." In winter the cold air in the long corridors, made more penetrating because of the interrupted sleep, made the young novices shiver. And after the chanting of Matins and the prayers in honor of the Blessed Virgin Mary, the novices were usually unable to get back to sleep. The hour for rising in the morning was five o'clock. They had only a few moments to make their beds, wash themselves and then hasten to church for the meditation period that preceded the daily Mass.

At eight o'clock they ate a light breakfast, which was followed by the study of the Rule and Constitutions. During the entire year of novitiate they were restricted to the reading and re-reading of those texts. No other reading material, sacred or profane, was permitted. Consequently, they were able to learn the will of their Seraphic Father St. Francis regarding the observance of the Rule and how to do it in the most perfect manner possible. In this way they strove to distance themselves completely from the things of this world, to practice "blind" obedience to their superiors and to die to self.

The rest of the morning was spent in the performance of various assigned duties in the church or in the monastery, cleaning their cells or doing the laundry. All this was done as they silently prayed *Ave Maria's*. Absolute silence prevailed and they were trained to keep their eyes lowered. Verbal communication was replaced by signs and gestures which were more or less intelligible.

The main meal, also very frugal, was served at noon. This was followed by a walk around the garden, then study, meditation and the recitation of the rosary.

Without a true vocation, it is not likely that any young man could stand this type of life for very long. As a matter of fact, after a month, Vincenzo Masone decided that he could not do it anymore and he returned to Pietrelcina. Fra Anastasio (in the world, Giovanni Di Carlo) was also on the verge of leaving. He told Fra Pio: "This life is too hard; it's not for us! Here they do penance constantly, day and night... Should we leave? I have already decided to go; and you?"

Francesco was astonished at such a question, which to him seemed insane and even diabolical. So he immediately replied: "What are you saying? After we have tried so hard to come here, should we leave? And what will our parents say, and all those who have helped us to come here? Ah, no; never!

Little by little, with the help of the Madonna and St. Francis, we shall get accustomed to it, as the others have done. Were not all who live in this monastery, and others as well, once like ourselves? No one is born a monk!"

Giovanni remained in the monastery. Years later, as Padre Anastasio, he gave heartfelt thanks to Padre Pio for the encouragement he received.

All his life, Padre Pio remembered that year of novitiate. During recreation periods he would often tell the younger friars about the novitiate as it was in his time. What remained most vividly in his memory was how much he suffered from the cold. He had only one worn-out woolen shirt in the shape of a chasuble under his Capuchin habit, and bare feet in sandals. In the cells and in the corridors there was no heat whatever; in the winter everything was frozen. Only with explicit permission of the master could a novice warm himself at the community fireplace.

On Monday, Wednesday and Friday, the novices "took the discipline." This took place before supper on those assigned days, with the whole community assembled in choir. After the entire community had recited the prescribed prayers, the lights were extinguished and the friars pulled their tunics up over their backs and would whip themselves with a small chain as they recited the *Miserere* and meditated on the Passion of Christ. Each one was supposed to "meditate piously on the sweet Son of God tied to the pillar, in order to share to some degree in his sufferings." The more fervent friars actually caused the blood to ooze from their skin.

In addition to this, fasting was prescribed for every Friday throughout the year; in the period from Epiphany (January 6) until Mardi Gras, all during Lent; and in preparation for Christmas from November 2 until December 24. On the vigils of the feasts of the Madonna and the Franciscan saints the main meal at noon was eaten on one's knees.

But what was a real affliction for Fra Pio was to have to witness the punishment of confreres who had committed some infraction against the Rule. For a second infraction the master imposed the discipline or the wearing of a wooden collar or a black bandage over the eyes. The methods may seem questionable to some, but they did enable the friar to practice patience, obedience and total annihilation of egoism.

In those days it was also forbidden to have frequent correspondence with family or friends. Before taking their place in the refectory, the novices had to kneel and, one after the other, accuse themselves of any faults to the superior and ask pardon with the word: *"Benedicite, Padre!"* ("Bless me, Father"). The superior then assigned a penance to each one and the novices would take their assigned places as they recited the prayer before the meal with the community. Then, seated, they listened to the reading of a passage from the Gospel. On feast days the superior could give permission for conversation during the meal, but it had to be moderate and only with the nearest companions. On other days the community listened to the reading from a spiritual book and the novices took turns doing the reading.

If a novice had need of something during the meal, he was to turn towards the superior and say: *"Benedicite, Padre,"* and wait for permission to make his request.

On one occasion a novice from Naples used the prescribed formula but received no response. Since he had already decided to leave the monastery, he asserted with impatience: "In Naples, to see insane people, you pay ten *soldi*. But here you can see them for free." He received the discipline for that remark and shortly thereafter he went back home.

Fra Pio was also punished one day. He had been given the assignment as sacristan. Because something needed was missing, not through his fault but because of the neglect of the one who had preceded him in that duty, he was deprived of Communion. The master was celebrating the Mass and, when he came to Fra Pio, he passed him by, saying: "The next time you will remember." Fra Pio suffered a great deal interiorly because of that undeserved punishment.

The novices were required to keep their eyes cast down. Fra Pio obeyed this rule literally. He would not even look up at the ceiling of the church or the roof of the monastery. With an incredible will power, he resisted every inclination to look up. One day his father, who had returned from America, and his brother Michele, came to visit him. Fra Pio went down with the master of novices to see his relatives, but because it was forbidden to speak or raise one's eyes without permission of the master, he just stood there in silence, looking down at the floor. Grazio thought that his son had become something of an imbecile. Fra Pio, on the other hand, wanted to embrace his father, but he had not yet received permission. Excitedly, his father turned to the master of novices and asked: "What have you done to my son? He does not recognize me anymore!"

Then Padre Tommaso said: "Fra Pio, you have permission…" Immediately, Francesco stood up and embraced his father, saying: "Papa! Papa!" Then he also greeted his brother Michele.

If the time spent in the novitiate left an indelible impression on the mind and soul of Padre Pio, the comportment, example, spirit of obedience, prayer and mortification of the young Capuchin likewise left its unforgettable mark on the memory of the friars who lived in close contact with him from January 22, 1903, until January 22, 1904. Padre Raffaele wrote later on:

> The master of novices, who had a sharp eye for discerning true vocations, has recounted more than once when I lived with him that Fra Pio was always an exemplary novice. Unlike the others, he was punctual in observance and precise in everything, so that he never gave the slightest reason to be corrected… For Fra Pio the greatest mortification was the refectory. At table he had to tell the master or the superior if he wanted to leave any food on his plate. This was a torment for him, so sometimes he played a shrewd game, and he did so without malice but in all simplicity. The community did not consider leaving food on one's plate to be a suitable

mortification. So if rice, minestrone or pasta was passed around in a large serving bowl, he could cleverly pass a helping to the novice next to him and leave his own bowl empty. But when the meal was served in individual prepared plates, and the superiors could easily control the situation, he would have to rise and ask permission to leave the pasta, the portion of food or the fruit or whatever was visible on his plate. This was a great mortification for him because he would have to give a reason in front of the whole community. Fortunately, the superior and the master of novices understood, so they left him in peace.

In addition to his spirit of mortification, Fra Pio was also exemplary in obedience and in the practice of prayer. Padre Guglielmo, who was in the novitiate with Fra Pio, stated:

> In the few months that he preceded me, it seemed to me that he had already made great progress in the religious life. His docility and respect for the voice of the superior were exceedingly prompt. His response was always, "Yes, Father," as he immediately set out to do what had been commanded... He was so observant of the silence required that it was impossible ever to hear a word from his mouth; and if sometimes it was necessary to explain some important matter to a confrere or reveal their defects or shortcomings, he would do so by gestures, by the expression on his face, or by his behavior.
>
> After the reading of a meditation on the Passion of our Lord Jesus Christ, he remained on his knees for the prescribed time and even longer when it was possible. He would often be visibly moved during the recitation of the prayers that were said while walking through the corridors, on the garden paths or elsewhere. In order to prolong his time of prayer, he would frequently ask permission to be dispensed from recreation, from the community walk, and sometimes even from supper... He was the first to make any gesture of adoration or

reverent genuflections before the Blessed Sacrament, the statue of the Blessed Virgin and the saints, and to urge his confreres by actions and gestures not to fail in these important duties.

Another companion from novitiate days, Padre Placido, noted regarding Fra Pio's prayer that his meditations were always on the sufferings of Jesus Crucified.

Towards the middle of November in 1903, the superiors assigned Fra Pio to instruct a young novice named Fra Angelico. The younger novice had a great admiration for the human and religious gifts of his older confrere and later wrote as follows:

A few days after I was vested in the Capuchin habit in the novitiate in Morcone, I was assigned to the care of a novice a few months older than me in the religious life, Fra Pio of Pietrelcina. I received from him my first lessons on religious life, which constitute the formation in the new environment in which the aspirant to the priesthood must develop his vocation and form himself in Capuchin spirituality.

I remember as if it were today that every day for about three months the good Fra Pio came to my cell to teach me about the required prayers, to explain the points of the Rule and Constitutions, to speak words of encouragement, especially when he knew instinctively that because of circumstances that even I was unable to understand, my vocation was vacillating because of nostalgia or yearning for freedom, all of which can be a test for a youth in full adolescence. I was then scarcely fifteen years old, at the mercy of all the fantasies that the imagination can produce. I waited with eagerness for the hour set by the master of novices for Fra Pio to encourage me with the words of a good confrere, to strengthen my vocation with the luminous ray of comfort, giving incentives for the priestly ministry and apostolate to which the two of us, each in his own way, had been called by the Lord for the reorganization and development of the Province.

I still keep in my heart the memory of the kindness and affability of Fra Pio, who since that time has presented himself to me suffused with a deep and unmistakable piety that is able to win the hearts of others... He impressed all of us novices by his impeccable comportment and the attraction that he exerted on all who came into contact with him.

That sweetness of character, that affability, was reserved by Fra Pio for his confreres. He tried to exercise a complete control over all his affections and to distance himself from the things of the world. He practiced a strict reserve that was not in keeping with his natural temperament, as is evident in this incident concerning his own mother.

One day Mamma Peppa left Pietrelcina with a packet of sweets for her Francesco. She longed to embrace him, for only a few months had passed since he had left home, but to her it seemed like an eternity. Her heart beating with anxiety and emotion, she knocked at the door of the monastery. A friar took her to the visitor's parlor while she awaited the arrival of her son. He appeared shortly thereafter with a companion. His mother's effusive greeting was met by reserve, coldness, and almost indifference on the part of her son. He stood there with his eyes cast down and his hands in the sleeves of his tunic.

Disturbed and not a little hurt, Mamma Peppa tried to offer Fra Pio the sweets that she had lovingly prepared for him and she said: "Franci, you are happy? I came all the way here to see you... to see if you are content... if you need anything."

"I'm all right, mamma," Francesco replied. "I don't need anything."

Sad and disappointed at the way her son received her, Giuseppa went back home. She confided in a friend and after describing the reception she received, she said: "Had I known he would act that way, I never would have gone."

The good woman did not understand that the behavior of her Francesco was an outward manifestation of his interior mortification. He was repressing a feeling which naturally wanted to express itself.

At the beginning of 1904, the community at Morcone in three ballotings and with unanimous approval declared that Fra Pio was worthy of living the Capuchin life. He immediately entered upon a spiritual retreat to prepare himself for religious profession. Padre Guglielmo has noted in this regard:

> I cannot forget the nine days preceding his religious profession, marked by so many practices of piety, prayers and tears, to prepare himself so that he would be worthy at the solemn moment in which he would make the promise of vows which certainly in his mind he intended to make perpetual. This is evident from the great eagerness, the impatient waiting to present himself before the altar and to express externally to Jesus, to the Blessed Virgin and to his superiors what was already firmly fixed in his heart.

January 22 finally arrived. At 11:45 in the morning, surrounded by the entire community, Fra Pio of Pietrelcina knelt before the altar in the church annexed to the monastery, placed his hands in those of the Father Guardian, Padre Francesco Maria, and in a voice trembling with emotion said:

> I, Fra Pio of Pietrelcina, vow and promise to almighty God, to Blessed Mary ever Virgin, to Blessed Father St. Francis, to all the saints and to you, Father, to observe the Rule of the Friars Minor, confirmed by Pope Honorius, living in obedience, with nothing of my own, and in chastity.

To these words the Father Guardian replied: "And I, on the part of God, promise you eternal life if you observe these things." Then the community intoned Psalm 132.

After the ceremony, attended by Mamma Peppa, his brother Michele and Uncle Angelantonio, all in the community embraced the newly professed. His mother, her eyes brimming with tears, said to him: "My son, now you are truly a son of St. Francis, and may he bless you."

On that same day the superior, Padre Francesco Maria, as delegate of the Provincial, Padre Pio of Benevento, called Fra Pio into the library of the monastery. In the presence of two witnesses, Padre Tommaso and Padre Bernardo, in accordance with a decree of the Sacred Congregation for Regulars, dated March 19, 1857, asked the newly professed to answer truthfully and sincerely the questions to be put to him.

After swearing under oath and with his hand on the Gospel, Fra Pio responded as follows:

— that he has sufficient knowledge of the Capuchin religious life, the contents of its decrees and what he must promise and observe under simple vows;

— that he has made profession of his own will, sincerely and with the intention of binding himself to God by the three simple vows (on his part irrevocable) of obedience, poverty and chastity and to live the life of the Friars Minor Capuchin;

— that he did not make profession under threat, by force or deception by any person in the world or in religion, but that he made it of his own will to consecrate himself to God in the religious state and more easily attain salvation;

— that he does not have and is not aware of having any incurable illness or other natural, civil or canonical impediment that would be an obstacle to his profession;

— to subject himself to the rule of perfect common life as prescribed in the ordinances and decrees of the 65th General Chapter of 1886.

Finally, Fra Pio wrote out the following declaration in his own hand:

> I, Fra Pio of Pietrelcina, known in the world as Francesco Forgione, of Grazio and Giuseppa Di Nunzio, born on May 25, 1887, with permission of the Very Reverend Father Pio of Benevento, of the Province of Sant'Angelo, vested as a cleric in this monastery at Morcone on January 22, 1903, at nine o'clock in the morning, having completed the year of my novitiate according to the decrees of the Sacred Congregation for Regulars, have made this morning at 11:30 profession of simple vows into the hands of the Reverend Father Francesco Maria of Sant'Elia, with the obligation to subject myself to the rule of perfect common life, the fulfillment of which is prescribed in the ordinances and decrees of the General Chapter of 1886, and I declare that I have made this profession freely, spontaneously, sincerely and with full awareness of what I have promised, not being aware of any impediments that would nullify this profession.
>
> In testimony of which I sign my name: Fra Pio of Pietrelcina M.P.

Fra Pio had completed all the rites and formalities for the profession of simple vows, which are temporary, but which in his heart were already perpetual.

6

IN THE STUDENTATE

*A*FTER COMPLETING THE YEAR OF NO-
vitiate, the candidates for the priesthood in the Order of Friars
Minor Capuchin had to enter upon several years of study. On
January 25, 1904, Fra Pio said farewell to the master of novices
and his fellow novices and, together with Fra Anastasio and the
Provincial, Padre Pio of Benevento, departed for the studentate
at Sant'Elia a Pianisi. Padre Tommaso, the novice master, was
sad to be parted from that young friar whom he had treated
with rigor mixed with mildness and understanding, once he
discovered in him a marked inclination to pass quickly along
the paths of asceticism and mysticism.

The three travellers arrived at Sant'Elia in the afternoon
of the same day in a sleet storm, barefoot and numb with
cold. Fra Fedele was waiting for them and he immediately
took them inside where, after greeting the superior, Padre
Angelo, they went to dry themselves in the warmth of the
community fireplace and have something to eat. The other
students noticed that the new arrivals were tired and hun-
gry, so they did not ask them a lot of questions. To know the
names of the new students, they would have to wait until the
next day when, at the moment of Communion, the clerical
students would descend from the choir and go to the altar

barefoot. Then, on the sole of the sandals, which would be left in the sacristy, the others would be able to read "Fra Pio" and "Fra Anastasio."

Very quickly Fra Pio aroused the admiration of all his confreres. "He was always mortified, recollected in silence... There was no danger that he would utter an unnecessary word... There was something in him that distinguished him from all the others... He was amiable and he always knew how to say a good word; he would offer advice in a very pleasant way... He was characterized by modesty, mortification and great piety... He was reserved and had great self-control, but at the same time he was affable and a very tractable person. He did not look down on others." Such was the testimony given by those who lived with him in the studentate.

In this new location Fra Pio breathed the aura of sanctity left by Padre Raffaele, who had gone to heaven three years earlier. Even while he was in the novitiate, Fra Pio had heard the friars speak of him. Now he visited the room that Padre Raffaele had lived in and he read on the name-plate: "In this cell the Servant of God Padre Raffaele of Sant'Elia piously lived and died a holy death on January 6, 1901." Fra Pio composed his own salutation to the holy friar:

> O pure and chosen soul of Padre Raffaele, I was not worthy to be among those who knew you during your earthly pilgrimage, but I thank God that he has let me know the perfume of your virtues. Your life enraptures my mind and heart, and may it please God that even in some small measure I can imitate you. Now that you are enjoying the vision of God, pray for me and for our monastic Province so that your spirit and that of the Seraphic Father may always shine forth in us.

Fra Pio diligently followed the lectures of his professors but he also accompanied them with fervent prayer. A classmate of his, Padre Leone, gave this testimony concerning him:

He was a person of ordinary talent, but he always knew the lesson, although we had the impression that he did not study a great deal. Using one excuse or another, I would go to his cell and almost always I would find him on his knees in prayer, his eyes red from weeping. I could say that he was a student in constant prayer...

During the studentate at Sant'Elia he still lived the spirit of the novitiate. Once he did not appear for the midnight Office. I went to call him, and I saw him kneeling at his bed with a covering over his shoulders and immersed in prayer. I don't remember ever hearing him complain about the poor food, even when the monastery could afford to do better; he never criticized the superiors; and when others did it, he would reprove them or he would walk away.

Padre Antonino asserted that "during prayers at Sant'Elia, and especially after Communion, Fra Pio shed so many tears that they formed a puddle on the floor. When asked the reason, the friar always ignored the question and remained silent. Finally, as his spiritual director, I commanded him to answer, and he said: 'I weep for my sins and the sins of all men'."

The answer echoes the one given by the Poverello of Assisi to a person who asked him why he was constantly weeping. And like St. Francis, Fra Pio was experiencing during that period a great longing to evangelize the people in the foreign mission countries.

In 1904 the Minister General of the Capuchins, Padre Bernardo d'Andermatt, made a canonical visitation at Sant'Elia. The young friar from Pietrelcina took advantage of the occasion to ask to be sent to a foreign mission. The request was not granted, perhaps because God was saving him for a heavier burden.

On January 18, 1905, an extraordinary phenomenon occurred. It was the first instance of bilocation, and a month later Fra Pio described it in a notebook:

Some days ago an unusual thing happened to me. While I was in choir with Fra Anastasio at about eleven o'clock at night on the 18th of last month (January, 1905), I found myself far away in an aristocratic residence, where the father was dying while a baby was being born. Then the most holy Mary appeared to me and said: "I entrust this creature to you; it is a precious jewel in the rough. Work on it, polish it, make it as brilliant as possible, because one day I want to adorn myself with it."

"How is that possible, since I am still a poor clerical student and I don't know if one day I shall have the good fortune and the joy to be a priest? And even if I shall be a priest, how can I think about this baby that is far from here?"

The Madonna replied: "Do not doubt; she is the one who will look for you, but first you will meet her in St. Peter's…"

After that, I found myself back in the choir.

Eventually this written account was turned over to Padre Agostino, the confessor and spiritual director of Padre Pio. He jealously safeguarded it and many years later he gave it to the interested party, Giovanna Rizzani Boschi. She was born in the city of Udine on January 18, 1905, during the very time in which her father, the Marquis Giovanni Battista Rizzani, was dying.

Later on, in 1923, as a student eighteen years old, Giovanna accompanied her aunt to San Giovanni Rotondo for the first time. She stood in the midst of the crowd, waiting for Padre Pio to come out of the sacristy before going to his cell. At one moment she found herself in the front line.

As soon as Padre Pio saw her, he approached her and held out his hand to be kissed. Then he said to her: "Giovanna, I know you. You were born on the day that your father died."

Giovanna was amazed. Who could have told Padre Pio this detail? On the following day, after confession, Padre Pio said to her: "My daughter, you have finally come. How many years I have been waiting for you!"

The girl replied: "Padre, I don't understand. Maybe you have mistaken me for someone else. This is the first time I have come to San Giovanni Rotondo."

"No; I am not mistaken," said Padre Pio. "We already met last year. Do you recall? On a summer afternoon you came into St. Peter's with a friend, looking for a priest who could rid your mind of some doubts that were bothering you. I was that Capuchin friar!"

Thus Giovanna finally learned the mysterious events that were connected with her birth. Then she remembered.

Her father, who had joined the Masons, had been away from God and the sacraments for many years. Struck down by an incurable sickness, he lay suffering in his home on Via Tiberio De Ciani, No. 33. The house was under constant surveillance by Masons to be sure that no priest would enter.

Shortly before the marquis died, his wife, Leonilde Serrao, while praying at the bedside, saw a Capuchin friar leave the room. She rose to her feet and called to him, but he disappeared in the corridor of the palace. She had been in a state of severe anxiety. She suffered intensely from the thought that her husband's life was about to end and he would die without the comfort of religion.

Suddenly she was seized with labor pains and her baby was born prematurely. Later on, with her newborn in her arms, she approached the bed of her husband. Meanwhile, outside, the Masons were preventing the parish priest of San Quirino from assisting the dying man. Then the administrator of the Marquis shouted angrily: "Let the priest enter! You can prevent him from entering to assist the Marquis, but you have no right to prevent him from baptizing the newborn baby."

Thus the priest succeeded in entering the palace. After baptizing the baby, he administered the sacraments to the dying man, who asked pardon of God and drew his last breath.

The widow returned with her children to her parents' home in Rome. She gave her daughter Giovanna a good education, predominantly religious. But as Giovanna grew up and began to apply herself to higher studies, she began to be tormented by religious doubts that threatened her faith. That is when, on a summer afternoon, she went to St. Peter's. She went to the sacristy in search of a priest but was told that it was almost closing time and therefore it would be difficult to find anyone.

The two young ladies were about to leave when they met a Capuchin friar near a confessional. Giovanna said to him: "Father, I don't want to go to confession but I would like some explanation concerning the doubts that are tormenting me, especially concerning the mystery of the Trinity." To dispel the clouds of doubt, the Capuchin friar said to her:

My daughter, who can understand and explain the mysteries of God? They are called mysteries precisely because our limited intelligence cannot comprehend them. We can only get a faint idea by using examples. Have you ever seen anyone making pasta? What makes the mass of pasta? Take the flour, the yeast, the water. They are three distinct elements. The flour is not the yeast, nor is it the water; the yeast is not the flour, nor is it the water; the water is not the flour, nor is it the yeast. Altogether the mass is of three elements, distinct one from another, and it forms one substance. Hence, three distinct elements, massed together, produce one substance. With this pasta you make three breads which have identically the same substance, but they are distinct in form, one from the other. Therefore, there are three breads, distinct from one another, but only one substance.

From this example we move on to God. God is one in nature, three in persons, equal but distinct, the one from the other. The Father is not the Son, nor the Holy Spirit; the Son is not the Father, nor the Holy Spirit; the Holy Spirit is not the Father, nor the Son. The Father generates the Son; the Son is generated by the Father; the Holy Spirit proceeds from the Father and the Son. There are three Persons, equal and distinct, and only one God, because the divine nature is unique and identical.

Giovanna thanked the Capuchin friar and leaving the confessional, she told her friend that she had found a learned and wise priest. She wanted to wait and ask him where she could find him if she ever needed counsel or confession again. But the friar did not come out of the confessional.

The sacristan announced the closing of the basilica. The young ladies told him that they were waiting for the friar who was hearing confessions. Fearing lest he might inadvertently lock the confessor in the basilica, the sacristan went to check. Pulling aside the curtain, he looked inside and then said: "Miss, there is no one here."

Giovanna was puzzled and disturbed because she had remained in that spot and she did not see the friar leave. Now, at a distance of many years, she has found him again at San Giovanni Rotondo. Overcome with emotion, Giovanna asked him, weeping: "Father, will you take care of me?"

"Surely, my daughter," he answered. "You belong to me. You have been entrusted to me by the Madonna. Come often to San Giovanni Rotondo and I will care for your soul, in accordance with the wish of our heavenly Mother. You are the firstborn of my heart. Love Jesus and love the holy Virgin, who thought of you before you were born."

In order to provide all the details surrounding the extraordinary phenomenon just described, I have taken the reader far from the monastery of Sant'Elia. Now I want to take you back there, where Fra Pio had another unusual experience in 1905 which he himself describes:

> I lived in the friary at Sant'Elia a Pianisi during my studies in philosophy. My cell was the second to the last one on the corridor that runs behind the church at the height of the niche containing the statue of the Immaculate Virgin... One night in the summer, after Matins, I had the door and window open because of the intense heat. Suddenly I heard a noise which seemed to come from a nearby cell. I asked myself what Fra Anastasio could be doing at this hour. Thinking that perhaps he

was keeping a vigil in prayer, I began to recite the holy rosary. In fact, there was a contest between the two of us to see who could pray more and I did not want to be left behind.

The noise continued and was in fact becoming louder, so I was about to call my confrere. At the same time there was a strong odor of sulphur. I went to the window to call him — the two windows, his and mine, were adjacent to each other. Getting no reply, I stepped back from the window and was terrified to see a huge dog enter the door, with smoke coming out of his mouth. I fell back on the bed and I heard a voice say: "It's this one." While I was still in the same position, I saw the brute leap up on the window sill and from there to the opposite roof, and disappear.

7

PHILOSOPHY AND THEOLOGY

*T*OWARDS THE MIDDLE OF OCTOBER, FRA Pio finished his studies at the secondary level and was ready to move on to the courses in philosophy. However, the church and monastery of Sant'Elia were due to be restored, so the students were transferred temporarily to San Marco in the province of Foggia. There, in the church annexed to the monastery, Fra Pio would spend long hours in prayer before the painting of the Madonna. This was noticed by Padre Benedetto, one of the most prestigious members of the Capuchin Province of Sant'Angelo. He was professor of Italian literature, the sciences, oratory, painting, sculpting, and an expert on the intellectual and moral formation of the religious. He took a special interest in the young friar from Pietrelcina and eventually became his spiritual director in 1922.

Meanwhile, during their stay at San Marco, the confreres had a further verification of the extraordinary virtue of Fra Pio. In his written account entitled *Ricordi su Padre Pio* (Recollections of Padre Pio), Padre Damaso stated:

> As soon as the bell rang for choir, Fra Pio would respond immediately. During recreation the other friars would go into the garden without permission

to pick green beans and eat them. They would offer some to Fra Pio but he would refuse them, and with such grace that it aroused their admiration and sympathy... One evening in choir he was making mental prayer. I was next to him, on his right (I remember it as clearly as if it were right now). Prompted by devotion mixed with curiosity, I secretly touched with my finger a large white handkerchief that Fra Pio had lying at his right side. I was thinking of his gift of tears (they said that his eyes were affected because of so much weeping). I removed my finger and it was wet, because the handkerchief was soaked with his tears. From that time on I had a special feeling in my heart for the goodness of Fra Pio.

However, Fra Pio tried in every way to be a young friar like the others. On one occasion he played a joke on one of his confreres who was excessively nervous and easily frightened.

When the bell rang for Matins at midnight, I was accustomed to hurry and wash my face before going to choir. One night as I was leaving the lavatory, with my towel over my arm, I saw the nervous confrere approaching. I don't know what came over me at that moment. I took a few steps back and hid behind some candlesticks. Nearby there was a skull on a table, which did not bring joy to anyone who looked at it in passing. I began to make a groaning sound and involuntarily I made the candlesticks jingle with my elbow. The confrere, having noticed among other things the movement of my towel, gave out a cry and ran off in terror. I ran after him, calling him by name. I wanted to calm him down. But the frightened boy fell down and I fell on top of him. When I told the other confreres what had happened, they had a good laugh.

Fra Pio remained at San Marco until April, 1906, and then he returned to Sant'Elia. In May he took part in an outing for the students. Before gathering together at Macchia Valfortore, they spotted in the field some trees laden with ripe cherries. Seeing the expressions on their faces, the owner invited them to help themselves to the fruit and eat all they want. Only Fra Pio and Padre Giustino held back and were content to pick a few cherries from the lower branches. Then, seeing that many branches were being broken, the farmer finally said: "Boys, eat as many cherries as you want, but at least leave the trees!"

Fra Pio shared the sentiments of the owner and feared that the young friars may have compromised the harvest for the following year. However, in the next year the yield was twice as large!

From Sant'Elia, Fra Pio, together with his companions, was sent to spend some days at the monastery of Casacalenda. After attending the funeral of the mother of the doctor who took care of the friars, they decided to make a visit to the shrine of the Madonna della Difesa on the following day. Unfortunately, after an hour on the way, they were overtaken by rain and had to turn back. But Fra Pio, now weakened by fasting and penance, caught cold and became ill. For twenty days he remained in bed with a fever, cold and a cough. He would say later that it was at that time that the illnesses began that would plague him for the rest of his life.

At the end of September in that same year the friars wanted to make another trip to Santa Croce di Magliano. Fra Pio joined the group, but this time also a sudden downpour forced them to seek shelter in the house of the archpriest Don Prospero, who offered to Fra Pio, the most delicate of the group, a cassock while he dried his soaked habit. Having experienced bad luck a second time, Fra Pio resolved that he would never again take part in an outing.

He became ill once more and Doctor Francesco Nardacchione diagnosed him as having an infection in his left lung. His prescription: he must live in the open air of his home town. Therefore, at the end of 1906 the superiors decided to let the young friar spend a period of rest with his family in Pietrelcina.

On January 27, 1907, Fra Pio, together with five confreres, made profession of solemn vows at Sant'Elia, into the hands of the superior, Padre Raffaele, binding themselves forever to the Friars Minor Capuchin for the sole purpose of working for the good of souls and for the service of God.

On April 16, 1907, Fra Pio was called to Benevento for military conscription. He was declared fit for service and was classified for provisory unlimited leave. However, his state of health was such that he could not resume life in the monastery, so his superiors sent him back home to Pietrelcina.

The examination in philosophy was held at San Marco on October 9. Fra Pio did very well and was promoted to the study of theology. At the end of October he was sent to Serracapriola where he met Padre Agostino and Padre Benedetto, who would guide him along the ways of the spiritual life. Years later, Padre Agostino wrote in his diary: "I knew Padre Pio in 1907 when I had him as a student of theology at Serracapriola. He was good, obedient and studious, but sickly. I do not recall anything extraordinary or supernatural at that time."

Padre Pio always remembered Serracapriola because he got intoxicated there without drinking a single drop. He had been helping the friars to bottle the wine in the cellar of the monastery and he became a victim of the fumes. When he re-called the event, he remarked: "That was the only time in my life that wine made me lose my head."

Except for a short period in Pietrelcina, Fra Pio remained in that monastery until November of 1908, when he and his confreres were transferred to the studentate of Sant'Egidio in Montefusco in the province of Avellino. There he remained until early in 1909 when, again for reasons of health, he was sent to Pietrelcina. He was accompanied by Padre Agostino. Both the professors and the students from that period gave eloquent testimony about him. For example, this is the account given by Padre Bernardino:

> I had Fra Pio as a student at Montefusco. He was not
> an outstanding student. Among his happy, boisterous

classmates, he was calm and quiet, even during the recreation period. He was always humble, meek and obedient. It was said that he had the gift of tears, so the superior dispensed him from meditation, lest he wear himself out and make himself ill. He was already sickly and had to be sent home to take the fresh air.

This is the statement from Padre Ilario:

As a student at Montefusco I would be with Fra Pio in choir as he recited the Office of the Blessed Virgin and sometimes I saw him with tears in his eyes. He was sickly, of delicate health, frequently with a fever and suffering severe pains… There was a time when the fever and weakness were intense. The doctor prescribed various medicines and total rest. But these cures were of no avail. I shall never forget that one night, around eleven o'clock, I heard a loud noise from his room, which was next to mine. Immediately I got out of bed and went to my confrere's room. The door was partly open and I saw Fra Pio prostrate on the floor and he was groaning. With great effort I lifted him up and put him on his bed. I noticed that when he fell he suffered a light wound, which I bathed. Then I arranged his bed covers and kept him company until I saw that the fear had passed. I said good night and went back to my room and to sleep. In the morning, after I informed the superior of the episode, he called the doctor, who declared that there was nothing seriously wrong with Fra Pio.

When this confrere could not come down to the refectory, I would take the meal to him, but usually he would not eat even half of it. Seeing that Fra Pio did not improve at Montefusco, but actually got worse, the superiors sent him to his home in the hope that maternal care and the fresh air of his native place would help him improve.

And yet, Fra Pio did not show symptoms of any particular illness. In fact, Padre Paolino recalled that when he was with him at Montefusco, Fra Pio was "a chubby youth with rosy cheeks, who gave no sign whatever of the illness from which he suffered. He wore a silk scarf around his neck to protect his throat, and his entire being breathed goodness and congeniality."

On December 19 Archbishop Benedetto Bonazzi conferred the four minor orders on Fra Pio in the cathedral at Benevento, and on the following December 21 Bishop Paolo Schinosi conferred on him the subdiaconate.

8

ADVANCING
TO THE PRIESTHOOD

*W*HEN THE SUPERIORS SENT FRA PIO TO his home in Pietrelcina, they thought that it would be only a brief stay. Then, when they saw that it would be much longer, they advised the young friar that in order to receive the diaconate, he would have to take part in the spiritual exercises that were scheduled to be held at Montefusco.

Fra Pio obeyed, but his state of health remained a matter of concern. The doctors for the friars, foreseeing only a few years of life for the patient, advised the superiors to let Fra Pio live with his family.

Meanwhile, at Pietrelcina, with study, meditation and prayer, Fra Pio was preparing for the diaconate, which was conferred on him on July 18, 1909, by Bishop Benedetto Maria Della Camera of Termopoli. But Padre Benedetto, who became provincial of the Capuchins in 1908, did not look favorably on Fra Pio's living at home. As soon as the young friar's health had gotten somewhat better, the provincial called him back to the monastery. That lasted only a few days, however, because Fra Pio had to return to Pietrelcina, where his health always improved.

On September 7, 1909, the Congregation for Religious declared that in particular cases the ecclesiastical studies done privately under certain specified circumstances could be validly accepted for promotion to the priesthood. Consequently, on January 2, 1910, Padre Benedetto wrote to Fra Pio:

> If you experience a notable improvement in health by breathing your native air, continue as you are, asking the good Lord to enable you at least to study and to do what is necessary for your advancement to the priesthood, in accordance with the latest regulations. I don't know what the divine plans are in willing that you be forced to remain with your family, but I submit to them, trustfully hoping that the crisis will be resolved (*Epistolario*, I, 177).

As a deacon in Pietrelcina, Fra Pio assisted Don Salvatore Pannullo with parish activities. But he lived in fear that his deceased sister would come to get him before his ordination as a priest. Although Dr. Andrea Cardone, who was taking care of him, did not agree with the diagnosis made by his colleague, Dr. Nardacchione, he did list a series of symptoms from which Fra Pio was suffering: severe pains in his chest and in his back, vomiting and copious sweating, persistent coughing, migraine headaches, and high fevers that aggravated his deteriorating condition.

At that time canon law required that a candidate should have completed 24 years of age for ordination to the priesthood. Fra Pio was about 23 years of age, so he asked the provincial to request the necessary dispensation so that he could anticipate priestly ordination for reasons of health. On March 14 he again wrote to the provincial: "The idea of being healed, after all the trials that the Most High has sent me, seems to me to be but a dream, or even a meaningless word. On the other hand, the idea of death seems very attractive to me and very close to happening" (*Epistolario*, I, 180).

Towards the end of June, a new pain at the bottom of his left lung rendered Fra Pio incapable of any activity whatever.

It was only with difficulty that he could even speak. Padre Benedetto, meanwhile, obtained from the Congregation for Religious the desired dispensation which would permit Fra Pio to be ordained nine months early. In passing this information to Fra Pio, Padre Benedetto stated that he should return to the monastery at Morcone so that he could prepare for his ordination to the priesthood.

As usual, Fra Pio obeyed, but as soon as he arrived at the monastery, he became ill with a high fever and vomiting. Out of compassion and to avoid aggravating the illness, the superior, Padre Tommaso, immediately sent Fra Pio back home to Pietrelcina and then advised the provincial, who immediately wrote a letter to Fra Pio:

> I am sorry, but I bow down before the decree of God who... does not permit you to dwell in the cloister to which he himself has deigned to call you... I have written to the vicar at Benevento concerning your examination. The parish priest will instruct you on the ceremonies of the Mass and meanwhile he will arrange with the curia to set the date for your examination (*Epistolario,* I, 191s).

Fra Pio received some lessons in moral theology from his friend Don Giuseppe Orlando; and from the pastor, Don Salvatore Pannullo, he received instruction in dogmatic theology and the liturgical ceremonies. Then, on July 30, accompanied by the pastor from Pietrelcina, Fra Pio went to Benevento to take the examination required before ordination. He passed the examination successfully and the date for his ordination was set for August 10, 1910. Ordinarily the bishop of the diocese, Benedetto Bonazzi, would have conferred ordination, but he was occupied elsewhere, so he designated Bishop Paolo Schinosi, titular bishop of Marcianapoli, as the ordaining prelate.

The day finally arrived: Wednesday, August 10, 1910, the feast of St. Lawrence. Preceded by a subdeacon carrying the book of the Gospels, the procession of clerics entered the cathedral at Benevento and proceeded to the chapel of St. Mary, where the canons recited the Divine Office daily. With his face as pale as wax, Fra Pio kept his gaze fixed on the huge crucifix that dominated the altar. His body appeared unusually frail because for several days he had been suffering from a high fever. Not yet fully recuperated, he had made the trip to Benevento by night, accompanied by Mamma Peppa, his brother Michele, Don Salvatore Pannullo, and his uncle, Angelantonio Scocca. During the trip to the cathedral, Don Salvatore described the priesthood as "one of the great masterpieces of Christ's love, which on certain men called by God, confers a special character which configures him and makes him resemble Christ the Priest and enables him to act in his name and thus prolong his presence in the world."

The young friar listened attentively and truly felt as if he were dying. Because of bad health, he had asked for and received the dispensation to anticipate this moment by nine months. He had dreamed of this for years, and now he felt the heavy weight of the responsibility that is connected with priestly ordination.

When everyone is assembled in the cathedral, a priest calls him by name, and Fra Pio of Pietrelcina responds: "Present!" and steps forward. Then, as the cantors intone the litany of the saints, he lies prostrate on the pavement with arms outstretched, praying fervently. Next, he kneels before the ordaining prelate to be raised to the priesthood. As a priest, he will preach with the authority of Christ and proclaim God's word to all. He promises to collaborate in the prophetic, priestly and pastoral ministry to make holy the Church of God.

The "laying on of hands" by all the priests present is a very moving ceremony. The young friar is now no longer pale. On the contrary, his cheeks are flushed when the bishop signs the palms of his hands with sacred chrism. Then he vests the newly ordained in the stole and chasuble, and places the chalice in his hands. The entire assembly now chants the melodious hymn, *Veni Creator Spiritus*. It is a hymn filled with inspiring invocations.

To the ritual prayers, Padre Pio of Pietrelcina adds his own personal prayer, which he will later print on a holy card as a souvenir of his ordination to the priesthood: "Jesus, my life and my breath, today , trembling, as I raise you in a mystery of love, with you may I be for the world the Way, the Truth and the Life, and for you, a holy priest, a perfect victim." Under the impulse of the Holy Spirit, who had just been invoked, Padre Pio offers himself as a victim soul.

In the body of the chapel, sitting next to Don Salvatore Pannullo, Mamma Peppa silently sheds tears of joy at seeing her son at the altar and thinking of her husband, far away in America. At the end of the ordination ceremony, everyone kisses the hands of the newly ordained priest, and in America, Grazio Forgione was most likely drinking a toast with his friends.

Padre Pio returned to Pietrelcina that same night with his relatives and friends. When they entered their own neighborhood, where a cross had been erected, they were greeted by a band which had been engaged by Michele's wife. The band was directed by Giuseppe Crafa and it escorted Padre Pio all the way to his home. But on seeing that the music was dedicated to him, Padre Pio blushed with discomfort and out of humility kept his head bowed. The neighbors were lined up along the street, showering him with coins and candies. Arriving home, all the relatives and guests were offered wine and sweets called *raffaioli*, and the children were given cookies.

In the following days Padre Pio celebrated Mass in the little church of Sant'Anna and prepared for his first solemn Mass, which was scheduled for Sunday, August 14 in the parish church of Santa Maria degli Angeli. The preacher for this Mass was Padre Agostino, who spoke about the threefold function of a priest: celebrating Mass, preaching the Gospel, and hearing confessions. For the time being, Padre Pio could exercise only one of those functions: celebration of Mass. At the end of the solemn Mass, memento cards were distributed to the people. They had been prepared by the provincial, Padre Benedetto, who had the following dedication printed on the cards:

To the beloved student of the Capuchins of Sant'Angelo, dear Padre Pio of Pietrelcina, on the joyful occasion of the first solemn Mass, hoping that God will possess him in heaven as he holds God in his hands on earth, praying that he will be mindful of him who has guided his affections. Fra Benedetto of San Marco in Lamis, Minister Provincial, Benevento, Feast of San Lorenzo. August 10, 1910.

9

FAR FROM THE CLOISTER

*F*ROM THAT DAY ONWARD, THE HOURS OF every day were for Padre Pio a preparation and a thanksgiving for the eucharistic sacrifice. He celebrated every Mass with the same fervor with which he had celebrated his first Mass. In order to give him something to do, the pastor of the parish invited him to help in the parish ministry. So Padre Pio normally celebrated daily Mass at the church of Santa Maria degli Angeli. In addition, depending on his state of health, he would celebrate Mass either in the nearby church of Sant'Anna or, riding Mercurio Scocca's donkey, at the rural chapels of San Gennaro or of San Michele. Sometimes he travelled as far as Pago Veiano to celebrate Mass.

Before tasting "the sweetness of the immaculate flesh of the Son of God," fully aware of his human unworthiness, Padre Pio spent a long time in prayer. Sometimes he spent more than an hour in prayerful preparation. Soon the people, who had to go out to work in the fields after Mass, began to complain that they could not spend hours and hours in church praying with him. They approached the parish priest, who in turn asked the advice of the superior of the Capuchins. The superior went in person to Pietrelcina to check on the health of Padre Pio.

Don Salvatore, the parish priest, was then advised to make a mental command, asking Padre Pio, in the name of holy obedience, to shorten his personal prayers. The pastor thought that the Capuchin superior was making fun of him and he was tempted to respond in like manner. But he remained silent.

However, one day he decided to try it out. Standing in the church at some distance from Padre Pio, he mentally gave the command that the celebrant should proceed with the Mass. Immediately, Padre Pio obeyed. Amazed, the pastor repeated the experiment for several days and it always worked out perfectly.

After Mass Padre Pio usually remained behind the altar to give thanks. His internal and external senses were dormant and his soul was wrapped in an ecstasy of intimate union with God and sweet contemplation of the divine attributes. As a result, his body fell into a state of such total lassitude that one time the sacristan, Michele Pilla, thought that he had died. He was so shocked that he ran to the parish priest and told him: "Hurry! The monk is dead!"

Knowing that it is much worse to interrupt the activity of God in a contemplative soul than to disturb many ordinary souls, Don Salvatore replied: "Don't worry; he will come back to life!" Then, around noon, the pastor went to the church and mentally commanded Padre Pio to come back to his senses. The Capuchin obeyed, and coming out of the ecstasy, he asked the priest if he had seen anyone. Don Salvatore reassured him and then accompanied him back to the rectory.

Always affable and cordial, with bowed head Padre Pio would greet everyone he met on the street. But he was always happy when it rained, because then the people would be carrying umbrellas and could not look him in the face. But if necessary, he would not hesitate to correct someone when he felt it was necessary. For example, he was adamant that Sunday should be observed as a day of rest, and he would not hesitate to reprimand anyone who worked on Sunday.

One day he met on the street a former companion who had not seen him in many years. The man greeted him effusively: "Good morning, Don Francesco." The Capuchin replied courteously, "I am no longer called Francesco. I have been baptized anew and I am now called Padre Pio."

Meanwhile, after years of work in America, Grazio was able to send back to the family what he had saved. He felt that his son the priest should have a decent house to live in, so with the money the family bought a new house at No. 44 via Santa Maria degli Angeli. Between 1910 and 1916 Padre Pio spent most of his time in that house when staying in Pietrelcina. The house was a witness to countless supernatural interventions. Looking back on that period, Padre Pio once said: "If those walls could talk..."

Each morning Mamma Peppa would go to the house to clean and also to check on her son's state of health. Sometimes she would find him so weak that, very worried, she would ask him how he could go on. "Mamma," Padre Pio answered, "don't give it a thought. Don't worry about it. It is the Madonna! She has always helped me and she will continue to do so."

What caused the most strain for the young Capuchin during that period was the constant, debilitating diabolical attacks and the relentless temptations. He himself revealed these things to his spiritual director:

> I find myself in the hands of the devil, who is trying to tear me away from the arms of Jesus. O God, what a war he wages against me! Sometimes I am almost out of my mind because of the constant struggle I have to endure...
>
> Who will deliver me from so many temptations and so many afflictions?...
>
> The devil wants me for himself at any cost...
>
> The enemy does all he can to make me consent to his impious designs; and in a special way this evil spirit tries with all sorts of phantasms to arouse in my heart thoughts of impurity and despair...
>
> "Bluebeard" does not want to admit defeat. He has taken all kinds of forms. On various occasions he has come to visit me together with his minions armed with clubs

and metal instruments, and what is worse, in their proper form. Who knows how many times he has thrown me out of the bed and dragged me around the room?...

The other night was one of the worst. From ten o'clock when I went to bed until five o'clock in the morning, that evil one did not stop beating me. He put many diabolical suggestions in my mind; thoughts of despair, of ceasing to trust in God. But praised be Jesus, because I defended myself by constantly repeating: "*Vulnera tua merita mea.*" [Your wounds are my merits.] I really thought that that was the last night of my life; or, if I did not die, I would go insane. At five o'clock in the morning, when the evil one left, my whole being was enveloped in such cold that I was shivering from head to foot. It lasted for a few hours. I was bleeding from the mouth...

Late that night they began their attack with devilish noise. They threw me on the floor; they beat me furiously; they hurled pillows, books, chairs in the air while they groaned in despair...

But the house on via Santa Maria degli Angeli was also the scene of heavenly as well as the diabolical attacks. Padre Pio once described them as follows:

Finally the Infant Jesus appeared and I told him that I wanted only to do his will. He consoled me and encouraged me after the sufferings of the night. O God, how he touched me to the heart, how my cheeks burned, pressed against this heavenly Infant!...

This past night I have spent the whole night with Jesus...

Celestial beings visited me and gave me a foretaste of the happiness of the blessed...

O Jesus, the vision of you hardly ever left me. And when I close my eyes at night, I see the veil fade away and paradise opens before me.

While living in that house, Padre Pio had experiences of hell and of paradise. Under the impulse of love, his soul soared

to the heights of the mystical life. On November 29, 1910, he
wrote to Padre Benedetto:

> I come to you now to ask a permission. For some
> time I have felt the need to offer myself to the Lord as
> a victim for poor sinners and for the souls in purgatory.
> This desire has constantly increased in my heart, so that
> now it has become, I would say, an intense passion. It is
> true that I have made this offering to the Lord at other
> times, asking him to inflict me with the punishments
> that he has prepared for sinners and the souls in purga-
> tory, even multiplying them a hundredfold, provided he
> converts and saves sinners and soon admits into paradise
> the souls in purgatory. But I want to make this offering
> to the Lord with your permission (*Epistolario,* I, 206).

Padre Benedetto answered the letter on December 1,
1910:

> Make the offering of which you have told me. It
> will be most acceptable to the Lord. Extend your arms
> on your cross and, offering to the heavenly Father the
> sacrifice of yourself in union with the loving Savior,
> suffer, groan and pray for the sins of the world and the
> needy ones in the other world, who are deserving of our
> compassion in their patient and indescribable anguish
> (*Epistolario,* I, 207).

The offering was accepted by the Lord and Padre Pio suffered atrocious physical pains and tremendous spiritual sufferings. Consumed with fever and the love of God, he kissed the
hand of him who afflicted him and gave thanks to the Virgin
Mary for the strength and the assistance that she provided.

When the family was residing in the country, he would
walk slowly along the road that leads to Piana Romana after
the celebration of Mass. He always carried with him a prayer
book. Sometimes he would stop at the home of his Aunt Daria
to drink a bowl of fresh milk, but more often he would give

responses and advice to the people who interrupted their work in order to speak to him.

His favorite spot in the country was under an elm tree in whose shade he would spend the rest of the day in prayer. At the foot of the tree his relatives had constructed a lean-to made out of hay, to protect him from the heat and the cold night air. But even in this tranquil spot his conversation with God was often disturbed by the devil, who would take on the form of a large serpent or a huge snarling cat.

It was under that same elm tree on the afternoon of September 7, 1911, that Padre Pio had an experience that he could not understand or explain. In the middle of his hands there suddenly appeared what looked like puncture wounds, accompanied by sharp pain at the center. The pain was most acute in the middle of the left hand. He felt similar pains in his feet and he was greatly disturbed. He returned to the farmhouse shaking his hands as if he had suddenly scalded them. When his mother saw him, she asked: "What are you doing, playing the guitar?" Padre Pio embraced her without saying a word.

The next morning he returned to the country and, after celebrating Mass, he told everything to the parish priest, and then added: "Don Salvatore, do me a favor. Let us ask Jesus to take away this annoyance. I want to suffer, even to die of suffering, but all in secret."

Don Salvatore replied: "Dear son, I'll pray with you to ask Jesus to take away this annoyance. But if it is God's will, you must submit and do his will in all things. And remember, if this is for the salvation of souls and the good of the whole world, you must say to Jesus: 'Do with me what you will'."

Some time later, Padre Pio wrote a letter to Padre Benedetto in which he described the phenomenon and the accompanying pain. "This phenomenon has been going on for almost a year, yet recently there has been a brief period of time in which it has not occurred. Please do not be upset that I have not mentioned it to you before. The reason is that I had to overcome a cursed embarrassment to tell you about it" (*Epistolario*, I, 234).

Padre Benedetto responded: "My dear son, thanks to the divine goodness for the favor which you have indicated in your recent letter. The only recommendation that I can make to you is not to reveal anything to anyone, because *secretum Regis abscondere bonum est* [It's good to hide the secrets of the Kingdom]."

But what had actually happened to Padre Pio? Padre Agostino had repeatedly asked for information about the phenomenon but he did not receive a reply from Padre Pio until October 10, 1915:

> In your persistent will to know, or rather, to receive answers to your questions, I cannot fail to recognize the express will of God, and with trembling hand and with a heart overflowing with sorrow,... I am disposed to obey... Your second question, is whether (Jesus) has granted (to his poor creature) the ineffable gift of his holy stigmata? The reply to that question must be in the affirmative, and the first time that Jesus deigned to grant this favor, the marks were visible, especially in one hand, and since this soul was terrified, it asked the Lord to take away the visible sign. From that time on it no longer appeared, but the disappearance of the marks did not cause the disappearance of the severe pain which I still feel, and especially in certain circumstances and on certain days (*Epistolario,* I, 669).

That is why, on September 8, 1911, Padre Pio, fearing that the marks of the stigmata would again become visible, asked Don Salvatore Pannullo to pray with him that they would remain hidden from the eyes of men. This time also the Lord heard the prayer of his servant and postponed the realization of his divine plan, already projected for the salvation of so many souls.

Meanwhile, the inhabitants of Pietrelcina gave other indications that they were aware that the finger of God was upon their Padre Pio. In fact, they did not hesitate to speak with pride of their fellow citizen as "our little saint." But Padre Benedetto, who knew much more than was evident to the people, anxious to keep that precious "pearl" in a jewel box, went into action on September 29. He wrote to Padre Pio:

> Your staying with your family bothers me very much. I would like to see you not only at one of our friaries, but at my side so that I could take care of you, for you know that I love you like a son. Therefore, I believe that your living outside the cloister serves no useful purpose, because it is evident that even with that you are not improving. If your illness is the express will of God and not a natural occurrence, it is better if you return to the shadow of religious life. Native air cannot cure one who has been visited by the Most High. Whether at home or in community, your health will always be what God wills (*Epistolario*, I, 237s).

The following month he arranged for Padre Ignacio, superior of the monastery at Morcone, to accompany Padre Pio to Naples for a medical appointment. On October 11, 1911, he communicated his decision to his spiritual son in few words: "I think that you should go to Naples and stay at Morcone, at least temporarily, where I hope to greet you." But when, on October 19, he found his confrere ill in that monastery, he changed his mind. Now he wants to conduct him personally to the capital to get a "scientific opinion as to whether he can live outside his native place without getting worse." The two of them met at the office of the famous professor, Antonio Cardarelli, professor, surgeon and director of the clinic. After examining the patient, the eminent professor concluded that the end of his life was very close. He advised the provincial to take the young priest to the closest monastery because there was no time to lose...

Padre Benedetto immediately thought of the monastery at Venafro, but first he wanted to get a memento of his exceptional spiritual son. He stopped at the studio of Nicola Germoglio to have a portrait photo taken of Padre Pio. On the way to the studio he revealed his intention to leave Padre Pio with the community at Venafro, where he could attend classes in sacred eloquence under the guidance of Padre Agostino.

They arrived at their destination on October 28, but after a few days Padre Pio became seriously ill. He was not able to retain even a slight part of the little that he ate. For two weeks he lived only on the Eucharist that he received, because he was too weak to celebrate Mass.

The superior of the monastery, Padre Evangelista, became alarmed and worried, so in the middle of November he took Padre Pio to Naples to be examined by a specialist who, unfortunately, could say very little about the mysterious illness. The two friars stayed overnight at a hotel, and in the morning they went to the shrine of Our Lady of the Rosary of Pompeii. They both celebrated Mass, one serving as acolyte for the other. At noon they went to a restaurant and ordered a meal, but after Padre Pio swallowed a few mouthfuls, he went to the window as if to take some fresh air, and vomited into the flower beds outside.

On arriving back at Venafro, Padre Pio's condition became much worse and he was confined to bed for six days. Three times during that period he was visited by Doctor Giuseppe De Vincenzi and Doctor Nicola Lombardi. Padre Pio appeared to be in a cataleptic state, his eyes wide open and looking upwards. His eyelids remained immobile, even when the doctor passed a lighted candle in front of his eyes. All the symptoms pointed to catalepsy and Doctor Nicola Lombardi naturally made that diagnosis at first. But on subsequent visits, when he was able to observe the patient more closely, he noted that Padre Pio "had his eyes fixed on something, as if someone were standing in front of him, and he spoke to Christ, the Madonna and his guardian angel… After his conversation [with unseen persons], he closed his eyes and fell asleep."

If the superior then went out of the room and spoke to Padre Pio in a low voice that could not be heard inside the room, Padre Pio immediately woke up, smiling and talking as if nothing had happened. The doctor changed his diagnosis and decided that Padre Pio had not been in a cataleptic state but in a state of ecstasy.

Padre Agostino was a privileged witness of the ecstasies, which were usually preceded or followed by diabolical attacks. The ecstasies could last for as long as one hour up to two hours and a half, and they could occur two or three times in a day. Since Padre Pio spoke during the ecstasies in a normally loud voice, Padre Agostino was able to write down everything he said and later transcribe the material in a series of four notebooks. Of course, he could only write down what Padre Pio said, because he could not hear the other side of the conversation. These are a few examples of the words of love and tenderness addressed to Jesus by Padre Pio:

> O Jesus, I love you very much... I want to be all yours... You ask love from me, love, love, love!... Let us remain together. I alone with you; you alone with me... O Jesus, give me your love! When you come into my heart, if you see anything that is not worthy of your love, destroy it!... I love you! I will hold you tightly, so tightly!... I will never let you go!
>
> Jesus, do you wish to leave me? Stay for a little while longer. It is so sweet to be with you!... Where were you yesterday morning? Did you see that scoundrel? How he frightened me!... Jesus, don't let him come anymore. I would rather forfeit the sweetness of your presence than have that fiend come back again... Jesus, when you come into my heart, what food do I need for nourishment? Only love!... O Jesus, so afflicted! Tell me, who has offended you!... Have I offended you?... You will find your glory in me? In me? What glory?... Jesus, don't appear to me like that! You tear my heart to pieces!... O my Jesus! Lower that sword! If it must fall, may it fall on my head alone... Yes, I want to be the victim... Yes, I am weak, but you can strengthen me!

On another occasion Padre Pio had a vision of St. Francis of Assisi, who informed him that he would be returning to Pietrelcina. The young friar was sad to hear that and he said: "Seraphic Father, are you expelling me from your Order?… Am I no longer your son?… You tell me that I must go to that land of exile. It is the will of God? Well then, *fiat!*"

In the meantime the friar's health was deteriorating at an alarming rate. Fully aware of his responsibility, Padre Evangelista, the local superior, wrote to the provincial, asking permission to send Padre Pio back to his family home in Pietrelcina. And when no reply was forthcoming, he presented the case to the Superior General in Rome. Padre Benedetto was displeased that Rome had become involved in a matter that was subject to his own authority and prudent judgment. Consequently, on December 4, 1911, he gave Padre Agostino permission to accompany Padre Pio back home.

The two friars left for Pietrelcina on December 7, and on the following day, the feast of the Immaculate Conception, Padre Agostino and Don Salvatore assisted Padre Pio in the celebration of a solemn Mass. He celebrated the sung Mass without any difficulty, as if he had never been sick. But the question remains: why was it the will of God that Padre Pio be sent to that "land of exile"?

Padre Agostino tried to find out the secret reason, so he asked Padre Pio directly. But the friar simply replied: "Father, I cannot tell you the reason why the Lord wills me to be in Pietrelcina; I would fail in charity." And if Padre Pio remained silent in order not to fail in charity, we should do likewise, instead of creating hypotheses to satisfy human curiosity.

Several times the young priest asked the provincial for authorization to hear confessions, but Padre Benedetto always refused to grant faculties, either because of Padre Pio's poor health or because he wanted to be sure that the young Capuchin had the required knowledge and skill to administer the sacrament of penance. On December 17 the provincial wrote to Padre Pio:

And when do you expect to return to the cloister? By this time you have experienced your native climate and you have seen that you are remaining the same and not recovering. I repeat what I told you vocally, namely, not to see anything extraordinary or contrary to the divine will or even to the natural law in returning to the religious life, even if you are sure that it will aggravate your condition. On the contrary, it seems to me that you have spent enough time outside the cloister for reasons of health. Have we come to the seraphic religious life to live well and to remain in it only so long as we do not become ill and die? Then everyone ought to go back to their families when they get sick and no one should die in religious life. I want you to go to Morcone and serve as assistant master of novices (*Epistolario,* I, 439).

Padre Pio knew that the Superior General of the Capuchins would no longer allow him to remain in the world. Once when speaking of him, the Superior General had said that it would be better for the young Capuchin to become a diocesan priest. Moreover, Padre Pio knew that he was a burden on the community, and with heartfelt sorrow he asked his provincial to regularize his situation by seeking a decree of secularization.

However, it would take a long time to obtain that document, so Padre Pio was ordered to return to Morcone. He obeyed, but within five days he was again reduced to a pitiful state. He was utterly confused and suffered severe damage to his chest. When it seemed that he was at the end of his life, he returned to Pietrelcina.

Padre Benedetto and Padre Agostino spoke about his case to the newly-elected (May, 1914) Superior General, Padre Venanzio of Lisle-en-Rigault. Seeing that it appeared to be the will of God, Padre Venanzio decided to ask for exclaustration for Padre Pio but with permission to wear the Capuchin habit so that "he can pray for the Order, to which he will always belong."

But Padre Pio received that notification with a sense of humiliation at being cut off from the seraphic Order. Padre

Agostino consoled him by explaining that the exclaustration was *breve ad tempus, habitu retento,* which meant that Padre Pio was still a Capuchin; his exclaustration would be brief and he would still wear the religious habit. He would simply be given permission to live in Pietrelcina, outside the cloister.

Consequently, on February 25, 1915, Pope Benedict XV granted the request that Padre Pio of Pietrelcina be permitted to wear the religious habit while living outside the monastery for reasons of health. The document from the Congregation for Religious granted *"petitam facultatem manendi extra claustra durante necessitate, retento habitu regulari"* (the faculty sought to remain outside the monastery for as long as necessary, wearing the habit as usual).

10

RETURN TO COMMUNITY LIFE

*I*N PIETRELCINA THE PRIESTLY APOSTO-
late of Padre Pio consisted of an ever-increasing spiritual direction, including spiritual guidance by mail for persons intent
on striving for greater perfection. First and foremost was the
Franciscan tertiary of outstanding virtue, Raffaelina Cerase,
who began to write to the saintly Capuchin at the suggestion
of Padre Agostino, her confessor. Through the frequent letters,
Raffaelina was able to appreciate the charismatic gifts of this
extraordinary spiritual director. She also understood his unusual
situation in the Franciscan Order because of his health. Feeling
certain that Padre Pio would be of greater help to souls if he
were living in the monastery, she offered herself as a "victim
soul" in order to obtain from the Lord the definitive return of
Padre Pio to the cloister.

At that time the First World War was causing horrendous
slaughter. There were about thirty religious of the Capuchin
province who had been sent to the front, and the provincial,
Padre Benedetto, felt certain that in all probability the third
category, from 1876 onward, would be called to arms. This
probability was a source of anxiety for Padre Pio. His physical
condition and the likelihood of undergoing such a dramatic

experience so alien to his temperament and style of life, not to mention his need for quiet and silence, caused him a great deal of worry.

One morning, while going through the countryside, he saw a manifesto affixed to a wall. He stopped, read it, and immediately returned home in a state of extreme agitation. That was on November 1, 1915. He took up his pen and wrote to Padre Agostino, his spiritual director: "With today's military manifesto, the members of the third category, '86 and '87, are called to arms, and since I belong to the latter group, I am included... As long as the divine plan for me is carried out, I desire nothing more" (*Epistolario*, I, 684).

On November 6, 1915, he departed from Pietrelcina in the direction of Benevento. Crossing the bridge over the Calore River, he turned to the left, toward l'Arco Traiano, and arrived at the military post. A very gruff medical officer examined him and diagnosed him as suffering from tuberculosis. He was sent to the military hospital at Caserta for a second examination. Eight days later he was examined by a doctor who pronounced him fit for service. He would not listen to the Capuchin's protest but simply told him: "Go to your regiment and meet your new superiors!"

Padre Pio began to have his usual seizures of vomiting and sharp pains in the chest. In the midst of persons from every state of life and condition, he did meet some very kind and noble individuals who surrounded him with sincere affection and exquisite care. He was assigned to the 10th Company of the Medical Corps in Naples, and he reported there on December 6, 1915. He was still wearing his Capuchin habit. He had been exempted from military service on April 26, 1907, and placed in the third category. But now, in 1915, he had to present himself for military duty and be examined. Noticing Padre Pio's weakened condition and not wanting to take the responsibility, the lieutenant in charge assigned Francesco Forgione to a medical officer for further examination and diagnosis. On December 17 all the doctors involved agreed that the soldier, Francesco

Forgione, was suffering from chronic bronchitis and they gave him a year's leave of absence for recuperation. On December 18 Padre Pio returned to Pietrelcina.

The provincial and Padre Agostino, however, agreed that it was time for Padre Pio to return to the monastery. The provincial tended to believe that the young priest was being deceived by the devil rather than having a mysterious illness. Some of the other friars thought that he was too attached to his native soil. In either case, the provincial felt it was time to act.

Meanwhile, Padre Agostino sought the help of Raffaelina Cerase, who had offered herself to God as a victim soul if Padre Pio could return to the cloister. During the fall of 1915 she had had surgery for a cancerous tumor, but now, in January, 1916, the cancer had returned and she was bedridden. She was very anxious to have Padre Pio visit her in Foggia and, if he did so, it would be possible to assign him to the friary in Foggia. That is what Raffaelina had in mind: "Padre Pio *will* come here. He will hear my confession and he will assist me at my death. Make the superiors give Padre Pio the faculties to hear confessions. He will save many souls." Consequently, Padre Agostino wrote to Padre Pio:

> Raffaelina is seriously ill. When I went to Foggia last week, I saw that the poor thing was suffering very much. She told me that the illness for which she had had surgery has returned. Her sister told me that Raffaelina is not well at all and at the same time she asked me to write to you, because Raffaelina also wants a visit from you. She herself told me that before she dies, she would like to meet you and have a visit from you. And you, what do you say?... For my part, I believe that God wills it. He will give you the grace to make the trip to Foggia... Are you going to let Raffaelina leave this world with that disappointment? Isn't she deserving of this grace? Don't you feel any obligation towards this soul who has prayed and still prays so much for you?
>
> Giovina [Raffaelina's sister] tells me that she will pay for the expense of the trip. The provincial not only

approves but is quite happy about it. If you decide to do it, you need only advise me and I will meet you at Benevento (*Epistolario*, I, 730).

On reading the letter, Padre Pio felt the fire of charity burn in his heart and he could not refuse. He was suffering from influenza and promised that he would leave as soon as he felt better. He will be accompanied by someone in order to save Padre Agostino from any embarrassment. Padre Agostino had previously encountered opposition in Pietrelcina. The people were not going to let Padre Pio be taken from them. On one occasion, when Padre Agostino went to Pietrelcina, an angry man said to him: "Padre Agusti, you want to take away our saint, don't you? If you try, we'll punch you in the face!" That is not the only occasion that they threatened Padre Agostino with physical violence.

On February 17, 1916, Padre Pio departed from Pietrelcina. He met Padre Agostino at Benevento and they proceeded together to Foggia. In the afternoon of that same day, still with Padre Agostino, he visited the sick woman. Later on, Padre Agostino wrote in his *Diary*: "The meeting of Padre Pio and Raffaelina was of two souls who had known each other in the Lord for a long time. They exchanged few words in my presence or to the sister Giovina or the domestic, Rosinella, who was treated as a member of the family."

That evening Padre Pio stayed at the Capuchin monastery of Sant'Anna, which was very close to the home of Raffaelina and Giovina Cerase. Every day Padre Pio visited Raffaelina. He celebrated Mass in the private chapel and then had lengthy spiritual conversations with Raffaelina. Then, when Raffaelina went to God on March 26, Padre Pio began to think of returning to Pietrelcina. This was prevented, however, by the peremptory command of the provincial, who told Padre Pio that "dead or alive, you are staying here at Foggia!" He obeyed the provincial and turned in the few coins that he had for his return journey to Pietrelcina. Then he wrote to his mother, telling her to send his few belongings to him at Foggia, and to Don Salvatore, asking him to pray that he may be worthy of God and pleasing in the eyes of the heavenly Father.

11

THE FRIARY OF SANT'ANNA

*T*HE FRIARY OF SANT'ANNA AND THE annexed church were on the outskirts of the city of Foggia. From his cell Padre Pio could see the vast expanse of Tavoliere, green with vegetation and the budding olive trees.

He was quickly absorbed into his new religious community, greatly appreciated for his virtue and his joyful spirit. The superior, Padre Nazareno, referred to him in his *Notizie su Padre Pio* (News Regarding Padre Pio) as "very content, and took his place among the members of the community, with whom he was cheerful and witty." But after a few days his cheerfulness was replaced by a very high fever, vomiting and loss of appetite.

The superior sent for Doctor Del Prete, who carefully examined the sick man and discovered "an infection of the right lung and a slight murmur in the left lung." He prescribed medication and complete isolation. The superior received a second opinion from a Doctor Tarallo, who discovered in the patient the presence of a murmur due to "an infection that comes and goes," but he definitely excluded tuberculosis.

In time the fever decreased and the vomiting stopped, but Padre Pio continued to suffer from loss of appetite. At meals he would eat only a small portion and after a few forkfuls, he would pass the dish to his neighbor. The superior noticed the reluctance of the friars and as a precaution he forbade that passing of the dish to others for hygienic reasons.

Padre Pio ended up staying away from supper and remaining in his cell. But he was not really alone, because the devil was there in monstrous and terrifying forms. Every night he waged a fierce battle against Padre Pio. The first time it happened, the friars were downstairs in the refectory and they suddenly heard a terrible crash and resounding echoes. As one friar described it, it sounded as if a drum of gasoline had been dropped from a height and had crashed to the floor. Frightened, the friars hastened to his room and they found Padre Pio prostrate on the bed and soaking wet with perspiration. His face was ashen white and he was so exhausted that he could not utter a single word.

The superior, who was always insistent on preserving peace and tranquillity in the community, was worried about the daily repetition of these noises and disturbances. One day he asked Padre Pio directly for an explanation, and the friar told him candidly that the devil tempted him with all his power and there ensued a violent struggle between them, accompanied by a loud uproar. But Padre Pio always emerged victorious. Other witnesses of this phenomenon were Bishop D'Agostino of Ariano Irpino and Padre Paolino, a temporary guest at the monastery. The superior, Padre Nazareno, left this description of events:

> One evening Bishop D'Agostino of Ariano Irpino stopped here while on a journey and I told him about the strange happenings. He said to me: "Father Guardian, the Middle Ages are over, and you still believe in this nonsense!" All right, I thought to myself, he is like the apostle Thomas, who would not believe unless he saw… But he will believe! When the bell rang for supper, he went down to the refectory. I dispensed from the usual silence in honor of our guest, and while we were speaking, I heard the trampling of feet above us, which always preceded the crashing noise. I asked everyone to be silent and the crash occurred. The Bishop's servant, who was eating in the guest room, dashed into the refec-

tory with his hair standing upright and overcome with fear. The Bishop was so frightened that he did not want to sleep alone that night, and the following morning he left the monastery and has never come back.

Padre Paolino was passing through Foggia, and he had heard that Padre Pio was tormented with diabolical temptations and attacks that were audible. But he found it hard to believe; it all seemed to be exaggerated. Nevertheless, he eventually wrote this testimony under the title *Le mie memorie intorno a Padre Pio* (Recollections Surrounding Padre Pio):

> Near the room of the unusual confrere, I said to Padre Pio in a lighthearted manner that since I find myself near him, I shall stay with him in his room until suppertime to see if the evil spirit has the courage to come into my presence.
>
> Smiling, Padre Pio discouraged me, saying that he hoped that the phenomenon would not occur this evening. But I was insistent, and I remained talking with Padre Pio while the friars were eating supper. The time passed and seeing that nothing was happening, I said to Padre Pio: "You see? Up to now nothing has happened, but I shall not go to supper until the brethren come out of the refectory and go to recreation."
>
> I was thinking that perhaps the devil did not want to have any witnesses. I left Padre Pio's cell and headed for the refectory. I should not have done it!
>
> As soon as I had taken the first step down the stairs, I heard the loud crash, and since it was my first time, I shook with fright from head to foot. I dashed back to Padre Pio's room like a shooting star... I was truly shaken to find him extremely pallid as was always the case and I noticed that he had perspired abundantly. In fact, everything happened as they had told me.

The provincial was informed about the strange happenings at Foggia and he immediately went to the Sant'Anna monastery. After making the necessary inquiries, he went to Padre Pio's room and told him: "My dear son, these disturbances must stop at once. This is a religious community in which there are not only old men, who are not too frightened by what is happening, but also young friars, who are terrified and live in a state of constant nervous tension... Then there are also the friars who pass through, especially now during the war, and you know that they will not stop here unless they are forced to do so out of necessity."

"But Father," said Padre Pio in all humility, "you know very well that I am not at fault and I have nothing to do with what is happening... It is God's will that permits this."

"I understand that you have nothing to do with it," said the provincial, "but you can, and indeed you ought to ask God to fulfill his will concerning you as he wishes, but you should tell him that as your superior, and for the good of this community, I want to be satisfied in this, namely, that these noises no longer continue."

"I will carry out the holy obedience," said Padre Pio. "Let us hope that the Lord will hear my poor prayer."

As he had promised, Padre Pio prayed fervently in accordance with the provincial's wishes and the Lord heard his prayer. To the amazement of the community, the noises stopped and the community returned to its usual peace and quiet.

However, the attacks by the devil did not end. Padre Pio continued to suffer a continual martyrdom because of the enormous amount of good that he was doing. In fact, he began to be sought out as a spiritual director and to such an extent that he did not have a spare moment to himself. In addition to this, numerous individuals from afar began to seek his prayers and intercession before God, and with positive results. Graces rained down from heaven through the merits of this "holy monk." And while many souls received from him direction and guidance for their Christian living, he himself felt like a blind man immersed in the darkest night. He was a victim on the altar of holocaust. Heaven seemed closed to him with doors of bronze and a metal fist seemed constantly to push him away.

12

A FEW DAYS IN
THE MOUNTAIN AIR

*T*HE CLIMATE AT FOGGIA SOON AGGRA-
vated the weakness of Padre Pio to an alarming degree. The
suffocating heat of summer, which is typical for that region,
proved to be insupportable for the friar from Pietrelcina. Even
when he celebrated Mass in the morning, he was always in
such a state of drowsiness that he needed another priest to assist him and sometimes to shake him. During the heat of the
day he could not rest comfortably in any place. For a while he
tried to rest on a couch near the outside balcony but he could
not find any relief. So he would go back to his cell.

His good friend Padre Paolino came to Foggia to preach
the novena in honor of St. Ann, patroness of the church and
monastery. Seeing how Padre Pio was suffering from the heat,
Padre Paolino thought of taking him to the monastery of San
Giovanni Rotondo, which is 600 meters above sea level. But it
was not without its complications. First of all, Padre Pio would
have to be willing to go, and secondly, it would be necessary
to get permission from the provincial.

The local superior, Padre Nazareno, saw no difficulty in
giving permission. Then Padre Paolino had to invite Padre Pio,

whose first question was: "And Father Provincial, what will he say if I go with you?"

"What do you expect him to say?" retorted Padre Paolino. "We don't have to get his permission for a few days. To visit neighboring monasteries like those at Foggia and San Giovanni Rotondo, the permission of the local superior suffices. You are not going there to stay but only for a visit. I will accompany you both ways. I sent him a letter to inform him of our plan."

That was enough to convince Padre Pio. After receiving the local superior's blessing, he went off with Padre Paolino, and once he arrived at San Giovanni Rotondo, he was welcomed with great affection by the friars and the students. The date was July 28, 1916.

When Padre Pio went for the first time to San Giovanni Rotondo, the friary and the little church of Santa Maria delle Grazie were located at the top of a barren hill. It was protected at the rear by the Gargano Mountains. It was an oasis of peace at the end of a dirt road that was bordered by olive, pine and cypress trees. Imitating the solemn gestures of the friars at prayer, the trees raised their branches to heaven. A few shepherds tended their flocks on the mountainside. The air was filled with the aroma of the wet earth, and the silence was broken only by the sound of a bell tied around a ram's neck or by the murmuring of the breeze through the branches of the cypress trees, announcing the coming rain.

The locality was very good for Padre Pio. Immersed in deep prayer in the choir of the church, his exhausted body could be refreshed by the mountain air and his heart could be inflamed with love. In the peaceful, cool evenings he would remember Pietrelcina and Mamma Peppa. How often he would go to the window and trace in the air what looked like a blessing as he gazed into the distance.

After a week at San Giovanni Rotondo, a bit concerned at the silence of the provincial, Padre Paolino accompanied Padre Pio back to Foggia. But once again, suffering intensely from the heat, he wrote to Padre Benedetto on August 13 and asked permission to return to San Giovanni Rotondo temporarily because his fever, which he feared could be malaria, had returned and he was exhausted from the heat at Foggia.

Padre Benedetto granted the request and assigned Padre Pio to San Giovanni Rotondo provisionally. Then, in the month of October, after consulting with his advisors, the provincial went to see Padre Pio and told him: "Well, do you want to remain here or go elsewhere?"

Padre Pio answered: "It's up to Your Reverence to decide. I will obey."

The provincial was perplexed, and it was only when Padre Paolino insisted that his dear friend and confrere should remain permanently at San Giovanni Rotondo, that Padre Benedetto assigned Padre Pio to that monastery and named him spiritual director of the students in the seraphic seminary.

13

SAN GIOVANNI ROTONDO

*P*ADRE PIO WAS VERY CONTENT IN HIS NEW assignment. He was especially grateful for the peace, the solitude and the mountain air. This is the way Padre Paolino describes that period:

> His principal occupations were the reading of ascetical literature, and especially Sacred Scripture; the spiritual direction of numerous souls who sought his counsel by mail and whom, with permission of the superior, he answered; spiritual director for the students, whose confessions he willingly heard when asked and who listened attentively to his spiritual conferences, all of which were permeated with the spirit of love for the Lord and with the greatest religious devotion.

The pastoral duties assigned to him gave the new spiritual director of the seminary a chance to have a marvelous experience with adolescents and, knowing their particular problems, to work out a pedagogy for that specific spiritual level. The way of faith that he proposed to the students was both a provocation and a challenge. The seminarians opened their hearts to him and gratefully received the balm of his spiritual counsel.

Padre Pio instilled in them the noble ideals from which springs the *joie de vivre*. He always emphasized that it is much more important to "be" than to "appear." He always proposed to them the ideal of the total gift of self. He paid a great deal of attention to lofty aspirations and to the typical needs of young men at that delicate stage of life. He fostered "participation" and promoted healthy activities in which, on occasion, he also took part.

He discussed youthful themes in the light of faith in God and faith in man. His teaching did not follow any particular method or system, but was based on the example of his constant and vigilant presence. His weekly conferences were adapted to the particular needs of the young students and they constituted a truly spiritual enrichment. Padre Pio always favored time for meditation in order to better understand the Gospel message. In that way, trained as they were to listen, the young men would be more inclined to live the words of life in depth. Padre Pio ushered a new springtime into their souls.

Great indeed was the impression he made on the seminarians, for whom he offered himself as a victim soul. The "halo of his holy life" and the ardor with which he spoke of Jesus, the Virgin Mary, prayer and the vocation to the priesthood did not pass unnoticed by the young friars. Everyone admired and loved with a filial love his "sweet and firm, mystical and paternal" image. One of his former students, Padre Federico, wrote:

> He was always praying, night and day. His first rostrum for us was the choir, where he spent long hours every day on his knees, as a faithful adorer of Jesus in the Blessed Sacrament. In our midst he always prayed and responded with the rosary in his right hand, but hidden in the folds of his habit. In the refectory, after hastily but listlessly taking a few mouthfuls, he would resume praying. He used to say to us: "You will see that there are forty-eight hours in a day." In fact, he never left choir before midnight... His day was a continual colloquium with God.

In addition to the spiritual direction by mail with which Padre Pio guided souls along the pathways to holiness, the provincial wanted him to give occasional conferences to the Franciscan lay tertiaries in the monastery parlor. He accepted this charge, and every Thursday and Sunday the tertiaries gathered together for instructions on living the Gospel teaching. His first spiritual daughters emerged from this group: Rachelina Russo, Michelina Ginolfi, the two Ventrella sisters, Giovanna and Lucia Fiorentino, Maria Ricciardi, and Maddalena Cascavilla. In time many others were added to this number.

In his conferences to the group, Padre Pio would give the basic instructions for making progress in the spiritual life. Fundamental points that he insisted upon were incessant prayer, mortification and daily meditation on the passion and death of Christ. He was likewise insistent that his spiritual daughters should practice obedience, go to confession regularly and receive Communion frequently. He urged them to be examples of virtue, and especially of purity and modesty.

In his heart Padre Pio rejoiced in their progress and gave thanks to the Lord for the abundant fruits of his apostolate.

14

NUMBER 12094

*A*T San Giovanni Rotondo, a solitary place of peace and religious fervor, Padre Pio passed his days serenely, but that was to be of short duration. In fact, the year of convalescence granted him by the military authorities was coming to a close.

On November 28, Padre Pio returned to Pietrelcina to await the day of his appointment at the medical hospital. He wrote to some of his spiritual daughters from home, asking their prayers and any suggestions on how he could avoid the examination that awaited him. He did not want to shrink from his duties, but he did want the military officials to acknowledge his infirmities which would prevent him from discharging any heavy duties that might be assigned to him, obligations that would be completely alien to his own inclinations and temperament.

After two weeks of nervous agitation and anxiety, December 16 was set as the date for his medical examination in Naples. He was a guest at the home of Carolina Montanile, who was a native of Pietrelcina. On Monday, December 18, he was readmitted to the military corps. He got through the first examination, and the doctors, taking note of his illness, placed him under observation. On the morning of December 21 he passed a second examination and was recovering in the military hospital.

It was only four days until Christmas and Padre Pio wanted to be able to prepare himself for that great solemnity in prayer and meditation. Instead, he was far from the cloister and far from home. During the night of the Christmas vigil he participated in the Mass celebrated by the military chaplain in the chapel of the hospital. On Christmas morning the military chaplain celebrated another Mass and then the chapel was locked. But Padre Pio managed to celebrate the customary three Masses on Christmas Day because he had been celebrating daily Mass in the neighboring church, so he returned there to celebrate his Christmas Masses. Other priests, however, who were among the military patients at the hospital, had to be satisfied with assisting at Mass rather than celebrating it. This is the way Padre Pio later described the incident to his confreres:

> I was a soldier and I was at the military hospital in Naples for medical examination. There were many other military persons there for the same reason, and some of them were priests. On Christmas Eve we went to midnight Mass in the hospital chapel, celebrated by the military chaplain. After the Mass we had a short social gathering and then went to our quarters. Many of the priests among us were naturally thinking of the three Masses that they were allowed to celebrate on Christmas.
>
> Early the next morning, I happened to meet one of the priests in my division and he was so sad and upset that he couldn't hold back his tears. I asked him: "What's the matter? What's wrong?" But he couldn't answer; his voice stuck in his throat, so I asked him again: "What's the matter? What is it?"
>
> "Look," he began. "here it is, it's Christmas and…"
>
> It seems that the poor fellow had gotten up very early and went to celebrate the Christmas Masses. In the sacristy he met the daughter of the sacristan, who was a very officious and domineering person. She demanded to know what he was doing, and when he said he was preparing to celebrate Mass, she asked: "Did

you go to Mass last night? That's enough! What more
do you want?" Then she went on to explain to the poor
priest: "You have satisfied the precept. What are you
looking for?"

After telling me what had happened, the priest la-
mented with some emotion: "Just think! Not to be able
to celebrate Mass on Christmas Day!"

I felt sorry for the priest, but I had my own problems
to worry about. The military chaplain celebrated a Mass
at eight o'clock on Christmas morning, and after the
services the hospital chapel was closed. But I knew of
a secret door that led from the corridor to the neighboring church. And walking back and forth in the corridor
I saw a soldier, though he was in civilian clothes, and
I asked him: "Do you know how to serve Mass?"

"But yes, Padre," he answered in a Neapolitan ac-
cent.

The two of us entered the church and found that it
was completely empty, and the sacristy as well. While
preparing the hosts and the wine, I said: "The daughter of
the sacristan might come and ask what we are doing."

But in typical Neapolitan fashion, the soldier said:
"Padre, I'll take care of it. Don't worry!" So I hastily
vested and we went to the altar to start Mass. After the
opening prayers I had just gone up to the altar when
I heard the door of the church open and close. It was
the daughter of the sacristan and she walked up the
aisle and spoke to the server: "Who gave permission to
celebrate Mass?"

He responded: "The Padre called me…"

When I returned to the sacristy after celebrating the
three Masses, the daughter of the sacristan demanded:
"Who gave you permission to celebrate Mass?"

"The Bishop."

"But I have not given permission to any of the others
to celebrate Mass."

"You have done wrong."

"But didn't you go to Mass last night?"

"I heard Mass; I assisted at the entire ceremony."

"And isn't that enough for you?"

"For me it is not enough."

"And who gave you permission to celebrate Mass?"

"The Bishop... As long as I am not suspended, I have a right to celebrate Mass."

The next day the daughter of the sacristan came to me with a paten and, pointing with her finger, she asked, very humbly and politely: "Padre, look. Is that a fragment [from a consecrated host]?"

In the morning of December 30, 1916, Padre Pio was summoned for his last medical examination. They found that his physical condition was still seriously below normal, so they gave him another six months of convalescence. He returned to San Giovanni Rotondo on January 6, 1917. On his examination sheet they had written the diagnosis: infection in both lungs and chronic bronchitis.

On May 16, Padre Pio made the longest journey of his life. Together with Padre Benedetto, he accompanied his sister Graziella to Rome, where she entered the semi-cloistered order of Bridgettine nuns, taking the name Suor Pia Dell'Addolorata.

The six months leave for convalescence were completed on June 30, 1917, and Francesco Forgione reported back for duty. However, instead of being retained, he returned to San Giovanni Rotondo, "awaiting orders." In the early days of July he went on a pilgrimage to Monte Sant'Angelo to venerate the archangel St. Michael, to whom he was greatly devoted. He had suggested the pilgrimage to the superior, Padre Paolino, who organized it either as a reward for the students to mark the successful end of the examinations or to please his confrere. The group consisted of Padre Pio, Nicola Perrotti, who placed his horse and carriage at their disposition, Rachelina Russo, Vincenzo Gisolfi and fourteen Capuchin students.

They departed at three o'clock in the morning, and at the beginning, Padre Pio managed to do very well on foot. Soon, however, he had to ride in the carriage; and by the time the group reached Pantano, he began to suffer from an intense chill.

It was July, but his teeth were chattering from cold. In the early morning hours there was usually a great deal of dampness and fog in that area. The superior covered Padre Pio with a jacket and a shawl. When the sun finally burst through the fog, he recovered from the chill. He walked for a while in order to stretch and then he began the recitation of the rosary, followed by some hymns in honor of the Madonna and St. Michael.

When the group reached the shrine, the Capuchin students formed a single file and walked up the steps to the Grotto keeping time with the invocations of the litany. At the entrance they were all deeply moved by Padre Pio, who was walking with slow, measured step at the head of the procession. It seems that at a certain point, he remembered that St. Francis of Assisi considered himself unworthy to enter the Grotto, but stopped at the entrance and spent an entire night there in prayerful vigil. Padre Pio knelt down and, visibly moved, he repeatedly kissed the threshold of the Grotto. Then, after listening to the sacristan's explanation of the Tau sketched by St. Francis, Padre Pio prostrated himself at the foot of the altar in honor of St. Michael and for a long time remained in prayer and recollection. Because of the intense humidity, drops of water were dripping down from the overhanging rocks, but to the amazement of the friars, everyone's habit became wet except Padre Pio's. The pilgrimage ended with the celebration of Mass, a final salute to the archangel Michael, and a visit to a benefactor.

On August 16, 1917, the soldier Francesco Forgione received a telegram, calling him back to the military. Returning to the hospital at Naples, he was subjected to various medical examinations. The diagnosis was the same as before: infection of the lungs. He was transferred to the medical clinic for solitary observation, where he remained until September 4. On that very day he was judged to be capable of internal military service and was assigned to the Italian Medical Corps. A few hours later he had to replace his beloved Capuchin habit with the uniform of a soldier. He folded his Franciscan habit, wrapped the long rosary and the white cord around it, kissed it reverently and put it away.

Looking around, he had the feeling that he was in an insane asylum. Everybody was running around in a great hurry. The commands of the officers were preceded and followed by expressions that wounded his sensibility. When reprimanded or corrected, the soldiers were ridiculed in such a way that caused laughter among their companions. The coarse language of the soldiers themselves was interspersed with cursing and blasphemy. Egoism ruled the day and good manners had given place to vulgarity and obscenity.

Disgusted with his surroundings, Padre Pio suffered a keen nostalgia for the monastery. In addition, he was very uncomfortable in the military uniform. His duties ranged from orderly, to messenger, to janitor. And he didn't always succeed in doing the work assigned to him. On one occasion he was made the object of the sarcasm, mockery and laughter of the other soldiers as he was cleaning the latrine. Mortified, he kept silent and fixed his mind and heart on God. He tried his best to adapt to life in the military barracks, but he was a misplaced soldier.

Padre Pio's health deteriorated more and more. He became weaker and weaker, so that it became evident to all that he was a sick man. One day he was sent to the railroad station to meet a group of twelve sick soldiers. When they reached the barracks, the officer in charge counted thirteen sick men instead of twelve.

Padre Pio spoke up: "No, Captain, there are only twelve sick men, not thirteen."

The officer said to him: "And you, are you healthy or sick? Aren't you the sickest one of all?"

He wrote to his provincial on September 19, 1917: "It is useless to tell you how I feel physically. I feel completely exhausted and if Jesus did not sustain me and come to my aid, I would certainly succumb. It would greatly displease me to leave this world because of this cursed fatigue, not from the cloister but from the barracks" (*Epistolario*, I, 942).

A week later, on September 27, he reported for a medical examination. Partly because of a slight fever that made him sensitive to the cold and partly to protect his clothing from his fellow soldiers, who enjoyed playing pranks on the recruits, he always wore all the clothing that had been issued. Consequently, when the officer commanded him to undress, he did so: first one jacket, then another; one shirt, then another; one pair of trousers, then another, etc. At the end, the surprised and amused officer exclaimed: "Forgione, you have not only removed your clothing, but an entire department store!"

The examining doctor had compassion on Francesco Forgione, and after reviewing all of his medical examinations, he declared him to be permanently unfit for military service. He told Padre Pio that he would willingly have placed him under medical observation, but it was necessary to wait a few days because there had been too many recently.

When Francesco Forgione was finally scheduled to see Captain Giannattasio, his illness had reached its peak. Seeing that the patient was seriously in need of care, he decided to send him to the main military hospital. There he would be assigned to the section under Captain Pizzini. The nurses in that section were the Daughters of Charity, and one of them, who certainly was not worthy of the name, tried to assign Padre Pio to chop wood, in spite of his weakened condition. A fellow soldier offered to take Padre Pio's place, but the religious began to shout at him. Indeed, she made so much noise that an officer, hearing the commotion, asked what was the reason. Then, seeing that the soldier Forgione could barely stand on his own two feet, he exerted his authority and excused him from the duty.

During those days Padre Pio had an opportunity to observe at close range the physical and moral suffering of the military patients and the treatment they received, which was anything but Christian. Possibly that was when the idea first germinated to do something for the alleviation of suffering and to found a clinic where the charity of Christ is practiced.

One of the doctors at the military hospital took notice of Padre Pio's condition and in the hope of curing him, he ordered special food for him, including chicken. Seeing that the chicken disappeared, the doctor was quite content, thinking that Padre Pio was eating it. On the contrary, the pieces of chicken ended up first in the drawer of the bedside table and later in the stomachs of other patients.

Finally, on November 3, after a visit from the examining physician, Padre Pio was granted a leave of absence for four months. Before leaving the hospital he signed a declaration to the effect that he would report back within eight days after November 6, 1917, and that he would have the document signed by the *carabinieri* at San Giovanni Rotondo after turning in his military uniform.

One of the soldiers went with Padre Pio to get the military pass for the train ride from Naples to Benevento. He also received one lira for travelling allowance, but at the train station, out of sympathy for a poor peddler who begged him to buy an umbrella "so he could buy bread for his children," Padre Pio gave him 50 *centesimi*.

During the journey to Benevento, Padre Pio was cold and feverish and, to make matters worse, the train was very late in arriving at Benevento, with the result that he missed the mail coach to Pietrelcina. It was two o'clock in the morning and the waiting room in the station was crowded with people. He thought of going into the buffet, where it would be warm, but there, too, the room was crowded, especially with military personnel.

At 3:30 a.m. the direct train from Foggia to Naples passed through, and a large number of people got on it. Then, at 4:00 a.m. another train passed through, and as a result there were empty places in the buffet. As Padre Pio sat down at a table, planning to order a coffee (he had only 50 *centesimi*), an officer and two soldiers entered the buffet and sat at a nearby table. When the waiter approached them, they ordered coffee, and when the waiter asked Padre Pio what he wanted, he ordered the same. The waiter soon returned with the four coffees and as soon as the three men drank theirs, they left. But Padre Pio did his best to stay in the warmth of the buffet as long as possible. When at last it was time for the mail coach, he went to pay the waiter for his coffee, but the waiter told him: "Thank you, soldier, it's all paid for!"

Wondering who could have paid, Padre Pio thought that "since the waiter was an older man, perhaps he recognized me and did me this favor. Another thought was that the military officer had paid."

Going out of the station to the place where the mail coach usually stood, Padre Pio realized that the fare was almost two lire, and he had only 50 *centesimi*. He looked around in the hope that he would see someone he knew and could borrow the price of the ticket from Benevento to Pietrelcina. Not seeing anyone he knew, he got into the coach and took a seat in the rear. He planned to ask the conductor to let him pay when they arrived at Pietrelcina, where he could get the money for the fare.

Meanwhile, other passengers were getting into the coach, and among them "a prosperous-looking man with a brand new valise, who sat next to me." After the coach started moving, the man took a thermos bottle out of his valise, poured out a glass of hot coffee and milk and insisted that Padre Pio accept it. At that moment the conductor approached them to ask their destination. "I had not even opened my mouth to respond when I heard him say: 'Soldier, your ticket for Pietrelcina is paid for.'"

When they arrived at Pietrelcina, a number of people got off the coach before Padre Pio, including the man who had sat next to him. Anxious to thank the gentleman, Padre Pio looked all round and even walked around looking for the man, but he did not see him. He had vanished as if by magic.

When Padre Pio arrived home that morning, his family had already gone out to the farm, and when they returned later in the day, they were anxious to see him in uniform. Instead, they found that he had already changed into his Capuchin habit. Nevertheless, they prevailed on him to get dressed in his military uniform, which he did to please them. "Now," he said, "you have seen *il pagliaccio* [the clown]!"

Although Padre Pio was undergoing physical and spiritual trials at this time, he nevertheless remained calm and serene.

He was anticipating the joy of spending Christmas with the community at San Giovanni Rotondo. But he had not forgotten his companions from the military, who at that time were at the front. In fact God permitted him to "fly" to their side and even to save a soul and a life. This is how it happened.

The supreme commander of the Italian army, Luigi Cadorna, was removed and replaced by General Armando Diaz, after the Italians suffered an overwhelming defeat in the battle of Caporetto (November, 1917). One evening, when he was suffering from deep depression, he gave orders that he was not to be disturbed under any circumstances. Unable to sleep, his mind was crowded with deep, dark thoughts. It was raining heavily and the claps of thunder reminded him of the firing of the Austrian cannons in that infamous battle. Going to his desk, he took his pistol out of the drawer and loaded it. He was fully intent on the desperate act of suicide. Looking up at that very instant, he saw standing before him the solitary figure of a Capuchin friar. He also perceived the aroma of roses and violets. Before he could ask the friar who he was and who had let him in, he felt someone embrace him. Then he heard a voice speak to him in the name of God, telling him to have courage and to put aside the pistol.

Immediately General Cadorna came to his senses and, ashamed of his momentary weakness, he wanted to speak to the friar, but he had vanished.

The General frequently thought about the strange incident, but it was only after the war, when he saw a photo of Padre Pio in the newspaper, that he recognized him as the friar who had mysteriously appeared and vanished. He wasted no time in going to San Giovanni Rotondo. There, dressed in civilian clothes, the General waited in the midst of the crowd. When Padre Pio passed by, he felt a sudden throb in his heart as he heard him say: "General, that was a nasty night we spent together."

On March 6, 1918, Padre Pio presented himself at the military hospital in Naples for his medical check-up. He received a favorable report for the first examination, but then he was gripped by an unusually high fever and was put to bed immediately. The fever was so high that it broke the thermometer as the nurses tried in vain to take the temperature of the soldier Forgione. He said to them with half a smile: "Don't try to take my temperature, or you'll break the thermometer. Then you will have to pay for it, not I!"

Finally the nurses had recourse to hot water thermometers and they registered as high as 48 degrees centigrade. The doctors were at a loss to explain the cause of the fever and they were amazed that a fever so high was not accompanied by delirium. They held a consultation in order to formulate a prognosis and after a microscopic analysis and an examination of his expectoration, they concluded that Francesco Forgione was suffering from an advanced state of tuberculosis and had no more than fifteen days to live.

"We are sending you home to die," they told him.

The diagnosis was changed on the following day to "double broncho-alveolitis." On his discharge papers it was noted that Francesco Forgione had served his country with good conduct, fidelity and honor.

Padre Pio went home to Pietrelcina, where he remained for only a few days. Mamma Peppa wanted so much to keep him for a little longer. She had not had time to do much for her son, who was so thin, so weak, so sick.

"I have to go to San Giovanni Rotondo," said Padre Pio.

"To die!" said his griefstricken father.

"To become a saint!" said Don Salvatore, the parish priest.

15

WOUNDED BY LOVE

*T*HE PROGNOSIS AND THE PREDICTION of the doctors came to nothing, as history soon proved. What had appeared to the medical staff as pathological was simply the effect of God's action, preparing his chosen servant for the reception of extraordinary gifts. Back at San Giovanni Rotondo, Padre Pio resumed his reading of spiritual books, the study and meditation on Sacred Scripture, the spiritual direction of numerous souls by mail, and the formation of the young aspirants for the priesthood.

Jesus had told Padre Pio in 1913: "Fear not; I shall make you suffer, but I shall also give you strength... I want your soul to be purified and tested by daily and hidden martyrdom" (*Epistolario*, I, 339). And now the state of purification was to reach its apex. In addition to the physical suffering, the Capuchin friar is to experience atrocious moral suffering, intensified by his own personal sensitivity.

We can get some indication of all this by quoting a few statements from his letters:

> I am always suspended on the hard wood of the cross, without consolation and without respite...
> How can I describe the agonizing pain which is causing my soul a martyrdom?...

My God, my God! Do not make me suffer any longer! I can stand it no more! I am suffering so intensely in my soul that I can say with the psalmist: "I have reached the watery depths; the flood overwhelms me. I am wearied with calling; my throat is parched. My eyes have failed with looking for my God" (Ps 69:3-4).

Padre Pio was tormented with thoughts and suggestions, with feelings of despair, with doubts as to whether he had corresponded with God's love, and with fear that he may have offended God, even in light matters. He no longer knew which path to follow in order to be united with God. He was afraid of falling into the abyss or of stumbling at every step; he doubted whether his sufferings were willed by God or even permitted by him; he was afraid that he had not sufficiently resisted the attacks of the devil or walked carefully enough to avoid his snares. As a result, his mind was filled with doubts and anxieties that kept him in a constant state of anguish.

He was experiencing the mystical purgation of the dark night of the soul. God was infusing his soul with a light so intense that it is purging it completely before raising it to the heights of mystical contemplation. But instead of illuminating his spirit, the bright light causes darkness and torment, so that he cries out in one of his letters:

My God! I have lost the way and I have lost you, but will I find you again? Have you condemned me to live for all eternity far from your face?… I seek God, but where can I find him? Every idea of God as Lord, Creator, Master, Love and Life has vanished. That is all gone, and I, alas, am lost in the folds of heavy darkness, searching in vain among the sparse memories for a lost love so that I am no longer able to love… O my great Good! Where can I find you? I have lost you, but I must find you because you are the life of my soul… My God! My God! I can say nothing else to you except: "Why have you forsaken me?" (*Epistolario,* I, 1028).

In the midst of his dark feelings of abandonment, Padre Pio reflected on his unworthiness and his moral misery when compared to the grandeur and holiness of God. He sometimes had the feeling of being rejected by God, the just Judge.

The encouragement of his own spiritual director was of no avail. He had written to tell Padre Pio on June 7, 1918, that it was not divine justice but crucified love that was asking him to share in his bitter pain without any comfort or any support except patient endurance. God, in fact, was in him, in his groaning, in his searching, "like a mother who tells her child to look for her while she stands behind him and holds him by the shoulders so he cannot turn around." So he has been transformed into a soul crucified by love.

Padre Pio always strove to live in perfect conformity to Christ. He wanted to identify with Christ as much as possible, to live and act as Jesus had done. As a result of this intense love for Jesus, he had such great empathy for the Savior that he had to all intents and purposes a perfect knowledge of the thoughts and affections of Christ. He himself had once said to one of his spiritual daughters: "To love Jesus perfectly, it would be necessary to be another Jesus."

But since love is tested in suffering and is proven by suffering, Padre Pio always feared that he was not suffering enough. Consequently, he could not love Jesus as much as he wanted to. He asked the Lord, therefore, to give him still more sufferings so that in return he could give him more love.

Gazing on the cross being carried by his Beloved, he realized its immense value. Jesus told him about his great suffering and, "with words that were at once a prayer and a command, he invited him to attach his body to the cross in order to alleviate the pain for Jesus." The desire to suffer in order to be purified yields to the desire to suffer for love. God willingly accepted this intense sentiment and bestowed on him the gifts of the Spirit: substantial touches, fusion of hearts, and wounds of love. On August 5, 1918, an extraordinary phenomenon occurred at San Giovanni Rotondo. This is how Padre Pio described it to Padre Benedetto:

I was hearing the confessions of our boys at five o'clock in the afternoon when all of a sudden I was filled with extreme terror at the sight of a heavenly being who presented himself to the eye of my intellect. He held some kind of weapon in his hand, like a long metal lance with a sharp point at the end, and it looked as if fire were shooting out of it. At the very moment that I saw all this, the heavenly being thrust the weapon into my soul with all his might. It was only with the greatest difficulty that I refrained from crying out, for it felt as if I were dying. I told the boy to leave the confessional because I felt ill and did not have the strength to continue.

This agony continued without ceasing until the morning of August 7. I can't tell you how much I suffered during this period. Even my internal organs felt torn and ruptured by that metal weapon... Since that day, I am mortally wounded. It feels as if there is a wound in the center of my being that is always open and it causes constant pain (*Epistolario*, I, 1065).

Padre Pio believed that he had been the recipient of "a new punishment inflicted by divine justice," but Padre Benedetto reassured him by saying that what had happened was not a "purgation" but a "painful union, and an effect of love."

As a matter of fact, Jesus had bestowed on the Capuchin mystic one of his most marvelous gifts: *the transverberation*. The term is used in mystical theology to describe the extraordinary phenomenon in which a spiritual being, such as an angel, is seen in an intellectual vision and seems to pierce the heart or side of a mystic with a lance or sword. St. Teresa of Avila experienced the same phenomenon and describes it in her autobiography (*Life*, chap. 29). Some authors go so far as to specify that the angel who performs the transverberation is a seraph, because the seraphim are angels of the highest order and relate to fire, purgation and flames of love. Although the pain of the transverberation is extreme, it is also accompanied by a sweetness and joy that can only be described as excessive.

On August 24, Padre Agostino wrote to Padre Pio: "From the evening of August 5 to the morning of August 6, Jesus gave you a proof of his special love for you... Have you not noted that August 6 was the feast of the Transfiguration of our Lord? Jesus wanted not only to transfigure your spirit, but to inflict on it a wound that only he can heal" (*Epistolario*, I, 1067s).

Padre Pio, confused, simply replied: "May he who caused the wound, heal it."

However, the transverberation was only the prelude to the stigmata, for it seems that God does not grant an extraordinary gift to the body without first preparing the soul.

Therefore, it seems that Padre Pio was now spiritually purged and strengthened, and was ready to receive the marks of the wounds of Christ. And those marks would, in turn, be a confirmation of his interior likeness to Christ.

Padre Pio had asked to share in the sufferings of Jesus and he had spiritually shared in the Passion of the Son of God. Now he could incarnate the marks of the Passion in his body and become, as it were, a living reproduction of the Redeemer.

16

ON THE CROSS OF CHRIST

*O*N FRIDAY MORNING, SEPTEMBER 20, 1918, there was no one in the friary at San Giovanni Rotondo. The superior was in San Marco to prepare for a liturgical celebration; Fra Nicola, assigned to collect alms, was out begging; the student friars were at recreation in the monastery garden.

Padre Pio was in the choir of the church, all alone. He was kneeling in one of the choir stalls, immobile, for he had finished celebrating Mass and was making his thanksgiving. His eyes were fixed on the huge crucifix, made of cypress wood, with lifelike features. The expression on the face was impressive, and even dramatic. The eyes, brimming with tears, seemed to beg for love, compassion, sharing. The blood that oozed from the wounds seemed to ask for more blood to be shed for the salvation of souls and for the world at large.

The clock had just struck nine. Oblivious to his surroundings except for Jesus crucified, Padre Pio prayed intensely. Wrapped in silence, he meditated on the mystery of the Cross. His internal and external senses, his physical and spiritual powers, all his faculties were suspended in a mystical quiet.

Meanwhile, the supernatural working of grace drew him into an ever more intimate union with God in an ecstasy of love. Then, all of a sudden he was granted one of the most remarkable prodigies in history: Padre Pio received the gift of the stigmata. Thanks to a letter which he wrote to Padre Benedetto on October 22, 1918, which was found among other letters in the care of Padre Agostino, we know some details on how the Lord impressed the marks of the stigmata on the Capuchin priest at San Giovanni Rotondo.

Padre Benedetto had heard some vague reports about something unusual happening at San Giovanni Rotondo. In a letter written on October 17, Padre Pio had mentioned something pertaining to what he was suffering at the hands of "a mysterious person." Consequently, on October 19 he wrote to Padre Pio and gave him a categorical command to explain what had happened. "My son, tell me *everything* and clearly, and not in a roundabout way... I want to know *everything* in great detail and under holy obedience" (*Epistolario*, II, 1091).

The substance of Padre Pio's reply is as follows:

> It was the morning of the 20th of this month and I was alone in choir after celebrating Mass, when I was overtaken by a repose similar to a sweet sleep. All my external and internal senses and all the faculties of my soul were in an indescribable quiet. During this time there was absolute silence around me and within me. There then followed a great peace and abandonment to total privation of everything... This all happened in an instant.
>
> While all this was happening, I saw in front of me a mysterious person, similar to the one I had seen on August 5, except that now his hands and feet and side were dripping blood. His countenance terrified me. I don't know how to tell you how I felt at that instant. I felt that I was dying, and I would have died had the Lord not intervened and sustained my heart, which felt as if it would burst forth from my chest. The countenance of the mysterious figure disappeared and I noticed that my hands and feet and side were pierced and oozing blood (*Epistolario*, I, 1093s).

In this letter Padre Pio did not call this incident "stigmatization," but "crucifixion." The terminology is not a simple euphemism, however. Rather, it refers to the completion and culmination of a previous mystical experience in which Padre Pio suffered the various stages of the Passion: the scourging, the crowning with thorns and the other sufferings.

Years previously, on February 1, 1913, in fact, Padre Pio had written to Padre Agostino: "When Jesus wants to let me know that he loves me, he lets me experience the wounds, the thorns and the agony of his Passion." On March 6, 1917, he confided to Padre Benedetto: "The heavenly Father does not fail to let me share in the sufferings of his only begotten Son, even physically. These sufferings are so acute that they cannot be described or imagined" (*Epistolario*, I, 335; 873).

Hence, on September 20, 1918, the "crucifixion" of Padre Pio took place in a remarkable manner so that, on the cross of Christ, he could participate in the redemptive mission of Christ. The awareness of what God was working in him caused him confusion and mortification. He expressed these sentiments in the letter to Padre Benedetto:

> Just imagine the anguish that I felt then and I still experience practically every day. The wound in the heart bleeds copiously, especially from Thursday night until Saturday. Father, I am dying of sorrow for the mortification and confusion caused by what I am suffering in my soul. I fear that I shall die from loss of blood if the Lord does not heed the cries of my poor heart and take this affliction from me. Will Jesus, who is so good, grant me this grace? Will he at least take away this confusion that these external signs cause in me? I will raise my voice and will not cease to beg him until, in his mercy, he removes, not the agony or the pain (which is impossible because I want to be inebriated with suffering), but these external marks that are an indescribable and unbearable humiliation (*Epistolario,* I, 1094).

But who was that "mysterious personage" with hands, feet and side oozing blood? Padre Pio does not identify him. He says only that the personage was similar to the one he had seen on August 5, the eve of the feast of the Transfiguration, when he suffered the transverberation. There are various hypotheses. For example, Padre Agostino wrote in his journal in 1919:

> On August 6, 1918, Jesus appeared in the form of a heavenly figure, armed with a lance, with which he pierced the heart. He physically felt his heart torn and dripping blood which coursed through his body, some of it coming from the mouth and the rest below.
>
> On the Friday after the feast of the stigmatization of St. Francis, September 20, he was in choir after Mass, making his thanksgiving. He was meditating on the Passion of Christ when that same heavenly figure appeared as on August 6, but this time crucified. He felt senseless and beside himself. There were five rays emanating from the Crucified, from the hands and feet and side, and they wounded his hands and feet and side. The vision lasted a few minutes and when he came to, he discovered that he had actually been wounded. The wounds were bleeding, especially the one near the heart. He was scarcely able to drag himself to his cell and wash his clothing, which was drenched with blood.

Padre Pio himself gave this oral account to his fellow countryman, Giuseppe Orlando:

> I was in choir, giving thanks after Mass, when suddenly I felt raised up to a level of ever-increasing sweetness that made me enjoy praying, and the more I prayed, the more enjoyment I experienced. At one moment a brilliant light shone on my eyes, and in the center of the light the wounded Christ appeared to me. He did not say anything to me and he disappeared.
>
> When I came to, I found myself on the floor, wounded. My hands, feet and side were bleeding and they were so painful that I couldn't get up.

What happened after this phenomenon, no one can say. One can imagine that on this, his "Good Friday," Padre Pio remained weak and confused. Not able to walk on his pierced feet, he would have dragged himself back to his cell. Perhaps he would have tried to wipe up any stains in the corridor, and once in his room he would have done his best to wash away the blood stains on his clothing and wash his hands and feet and side.

He must have suffered moments of indescribable embarrassment and anxiety. First of all, there was the natural fear of bleeding to excess; then the problem of keeping the signs hidden. Padre Pio could readily imagine some of the consequences: human curiosity, misunderstanding, false accusations, pain produced by the wounds. He turned to God and asked for help, and the words came to mind: "My grace is sufficient for you."

However much Padre Pio tried to conceal the marks of the stigmata, he did not always succeed in hiding them from the eyes of those around him. One of his early spiritual daughters, Nina Campanile, went to the friary on September 21, 1918, to offer a stipend for a Mass. Her sister Vittoria, seven months pregnant, had fallen sick in the flu epidemic which was raging throughout the area. Nina met Padre Pio in the sacristy and told him about Vittoria's serious condition. He told her in categorical tones: "Listen, even if you had seen her expiring, you must believe that she will be cured!"

Nina was reassured, and when she handed him the Mass offering, she noticed the mark on the back of his hand. Not wanting to say what her feminine intuition was suggesting, she simply exclaimed: "Padre, did you burn your hand?"

Padre Pio did not respond, but he put his hands behind his back. As she was leaving, she tried to take his right hand and kiss it right on the wound. Padre Pio felt a bit vexed and he said to her: "If you only knew the embarrassment you cause me!"

When Nina reached home, she told her mother that Vittoria would recover and that Padre Pio has the stigmata like

St. Francis of Assisi. The news quickly spread throughout the district. The next day Nina herself went back to the monastery and told the superior: "Padre Paolino, do you know that Padre Pio has the stigmata?" The superior smiled incredulously but because of Nina's insistence, he promised to investigate.

Padre Paolino was accustomed to go each morning to the cell of Padre Pio to chat with him for a few moments. So the following morning he went with the precise intention of finding out whether Nina's report was true. He entered the room without knocking and found Padre Pio busy writing at his desk. He immediately looked at his hands and verified for himself that what Nina had said was true. That same day he notified the provincial and asked him to come immediately to San Giovanni Rotondo.

Padre Benedetto, the provincial, wrote back at once and commanded that there be absolute silence about what had happened. He did not go there immediately but, as we have seen, he wrote to Padre Pio and asked for detailed information.

Towards the middle of December of that year, while Padre Pio was experiencing the bittersweet agony caused by the "loving wounds" that made him suffer and at the same time nourished his spirit, the "mysterious personage" produced a third marvelous effect. Padre Pio described it in a letter to Padre Benedetto on December 20, 1918:

> For a few days I have been aware that there is in me something that feels like a thin sheet of iron that extends from the bottom part of my heart to the lower right side of my back. It causes very sharp pain and doesn't let me get any rest. But what is it?
>
> I started to notice this new phenomenon after an apparition of that mysterious personage of August 5 and 6 and September 20, of which I spoke to you, if you recall, in my other letters (*Epistolario*, I, 1106).

Thus, in addition to the transverberation of the heart that occurred in August, there is now what he calls a "new phenomenon," which seems to have pierced — or better, to have slashed — his heart from bottom to top.

17

OBSERVATION BY DOCTORS

$\mathscr{A}$T THE END OF FEBRUARY, 1919, THE
provincial had gone to San Giovanni Rotondo to find out what
effects the experiences of Padre Pio had had on his body. On
the following March 3, which was Ash Wednesday, he wrote
to Padre Agostino:

> They are not marks or imprints, but actual wounds
> that pierce his hands and his feet. Then I examined the
> one on his side. It is a real gash which constantly oozes
> blood or a bloody liquid. On Fridays it is real blood.
> I found that he can stand on his feet only with difficulty,
> but he is able to celebrate Mass, and when he says Mass,
> the wounds on his hands are exposed to the public, since
> his hands must be elevated and bare.

Padre Benedetto also made an official report to the prepara-
tory congregation for the Capuchin chapter, which was held at
San Marco from May 4 to 6. He also sent a communication to the
Minister General of the Capuchin Order in Rome. He returned
to San Giovanni Rotondo on May 14 in the company of Padre
Paolo and Doctor Luigi Romanelli, of the civilian hospital at
Barletta, who had been put in charge of visiting Padre Pio at
the behest of Padre Agostino.

Doctor Romanelli remained at the friary until the morning of May 17. He went to confession to Padre Pio; he interviewed him; he attended his Mass and received Communion; and finally he wrote a detailed report on his visit. These are the pertinent points for our purposes:

In the palms of both hands and precisely at the level of the third metacarpus a simple observation revealed a red viscose pigmentation of the skin over a surface the size of a five-centime coin on the right hand and the size of a two-centime coin on the left hand. The marks were somewhat circular in shape and the edges were lightly outlined.

On closer examination, it was noted that there was a shiny membrane somewhat raised in the center, forming a little knob, from which extended thin streaks that were darker in color, tending to black. This whole area is higher than the surrounding tissue, which is solid and normal.

If the area is lightly touched, one doesn't perceive any resistance from bone or muscle. Rather, the membrane is distinctly elastic and there is no actual bleeding.

On the back of both hands the skin was the same as on the palms, except that it was not raised up and had no lines emanating from the center. Putting the thumb on the palm of the hand and the index finger on the back, and exerting a bit of pressure, causes sharp pain. Beneath the membrane there is empty space.

On the instep of both feet there is also a circular area the size of a five-centime coin, also covered with a bright red membrane that is somewhat shiny and well defined. Like the membrane on the hands, it is also elastic, and when lightly pressed gives the impression of emptiness underneath.

On the bottom of the feet there is a similar membrane, elastic and covering an empty space. But all the movements of hands and feet are within the range of normalcy.

On the left side, approximately at the sixth space in the rib cage, there is a gash, but it is difficult to estimate the depth or the direction within the cavity. The gash itself is like one caused by a stab wound.

All of these lesions date back to September, 1918. In my opinion, they cannot be classified as resulting from infection or trauma.

In the meantime, the press had spread the news that there was a Capuchin priest at San Giovanni Rotondo who had the stigmata. The news release also stated that he worked miracles. Almost immediately crowds began to gather at the church and monastery and soon there were organized pilgrimages. They included not only the simple faithful, but journalists, doctors, sick people hoping for a cure, religious and clergy, and the curious. The little monastery church became so crowded that the friars had to call upon the *carabinieri* for order and security.

In addition to this, the Congregation for the Saints was also involved, in the person of the procurator general for the Capuchin Order, Padre Giuseppe Antonio. He appointed Doctor Amico Bignami, professor of medical pathology at the Royal University in Rome, to visit Padre Pio and make a report. Accompanied by Padre Pietro, who had been elected provincial in July, 1919, Doctor Bignami went to San Giovanni Rotondo. He spent two days there and before he left, he ordered a very special test: the wounds were to be bandaged in the presence of two witnesses and left that way for eight days. During that time there was to be a strict control to be sure that the bandages were left untouched, and at the end of eight days the two witnesses were to report.

After returning to Rome, Doctor Bignami issued his statement. He began by stating that the lesions were the result of a pathological condition which could be explained in three possible ways:

1. They were deliberately and artificially caused;
2. They are manifestations of a morbid condition;

3. They are partly the result of a morbid condition and partly artificially induced. [Note that, at the time, Doctor Bignami did not even suggest the possibility of a supernatural cause.]

Without direct proof, he was unwilling to accept the first hypothesis, but the second one, at least in part, was worthy of consideration. Pathologists are acquainted with neurotic necrosis and with the pathological phenomenon of hematidrosis. Doctor Bignami concluded that the lesions on the hands of Padre Pio were caused by neurotic necrosis but he said that "with the knowledge presently at our disposal, we cannot explain the perfectly symmetrical formation of the lesions." Consequently, he concluded: "In my opinion these facts can be explained satisfactorily by the third hypothesis. In fact, we can conclude that the lesions described started as a pathological product (multiple neurotic necrosis of the skin) and then, perhaps unconsciously, by the phenomenon of auto-suggestion they assumed their symmetrical shapes and were maintained by the use of some chemical, such as tincture of iodine."

As regards the marks on the feet, Doctor Bignami stated that the lesions appeared to be superficial and that they were very likely the result of the repeated application of tincture of iodine. He went on to explain that the tincture of iodine becomes a caustic irritant after application, but many people and even some doctors do not know this. So it is natural that the application of tincture of iodine over a period of months would intensify any preexisting irritation of the skin or even affect normal tissue. "This seems to me to be the most acceptable interpretation of the facts that I observed. In any case, it can be stated that there is nothing in the alterations of the skin that cannot be explained as the result of a morbid state or the action of chemical agents."

At approximately the same time that Doctor Bignami issued his report, Padre Paolino, Padre Basilio and Padre Ludivoco submitted their statement:

We, the undersigned, testify under oath that having been commanded by the Very Reverend Padre Pietro to bandage the wounds of Padre Pio, Capuchin priest, we have verified the following:

1. The condition of the wounds during the eight days has remained the same, except that on the last day they were a bright red color.

2. Every day, as one can see from the bandages which we have saved, all the wounds shed blood; much more copiously on the last day, and to such an extent that we had to use a towel while he was celebrating Mass to wipe the blood off his hands.

It should be noted that in bandaging the wounds, we have not applied any medicine and, while we have complete confidence in Padre Pio, in order to avoid any suspicion, we have removed the tincture of iodine that he kept in his room.

In addition to the foregoing statement, we read in Padre Paolino's *Le mie memorie intorno a Padre Pio* (Recollections Surrounding Padre Pio):

For the space of eight days, every morning the bandages of the previous day were removed, after verifying the closure, and new ones were applied and in such a way that we had the opportunity to see and observe the wounds on the body of the Father, who suffered intensely in his heart at revealing the wounds which he always tried to hide from the eyes of all. Anyone who could have seen the face of the Father at that time would have been able to see clearly the great repugnance together with the pallor of his countenance, as I have seen with my own eyes. As a chronicler, I must say that what has impressed me the most in seeing the wounds is the one on the side of the heart, which is really at the heart and not on the other side of the chest, as I have heard many people say. It has the shape of an X, from which one can deduce that there are two wounds, and that would be in accord with what

I have heard, although I cannot prove it for lack of evidence, namely, that long before receiving the stigmata, Padre Pio had been wounded in his heart by the lance of an angel. And finally, another thing that has impressed me is that the wound has the appearance of a violent thrust that is not superficial but entered deep into the chest.

The interpretation of Doctor Bignami was vehemently refuted by Doctor Giorgio Festa, who studied Padre Pio between 1920 and 1925, and Doctor Romanelli. In fact, it was the Minister General of the Capuchins, Padre Venanzio, who asked Doctor Festa to visit Padre Pio. On October 9, 1919, the doctor met with the officials of the Capuchin Province at Foggia in order to have detailed information about Padre Pio. He then went to San Giovanni Rotondo to observe Padre Pio from both a medical and a psychological aspect. On November 15 he submitted his report to the Curia of the Capuchin Order.

Doctor Festa stated that "we are faced with an extraordinary phenomenon that we are unable to explain with the knowledge we possess." The lesions "are definitely not the result of a localized infection nor the manifestation of a constitutional illness." The wounds "have not been caused by any sharp cutting instrument nor by the application of a highly irritating chemical substance." In the latter case, "the lesion would not be neatly contained within a given area, but would tend to extend beyond the limits." Doctor Festa then concluded:

> The wounds which Padre Pio manifests and the hemorraghing that results have an origin which our present knowledge is unable to explain. The reason for their existence far surpasses human science. And if one thinks of the goodness, affability and gentleness of his character; of his life dedicated entirely to sacrifice and the good of those who come to him; of his lengthy vigils in meditation and prayer, it will not be so difficult to understand how his soul could become an authentic center of attraction for divine grace and how this could

have impressed on him the signs of his predilection precisely there where our Lord suffered the most cruel martyrdom. Hence, that which for science would seem to be an enigma, can be explained by faith.

On August 31, 1920, after a visit to Padre Pio with Doctor Romanelli on July 15, Doctor Festa wrote another statement in which he confirmed what he had already written in his first deposition and he challenged the statements made by Doctor Bignami. Later, on November 7, 1920, Doctor Romanelli also wrote a precise critique of the conclusions of Doctor Bignami:

> In trying to explain the persistence of the lesions, the illustrious clinician wants to attribute it to tincture of iodine... Is the professor forgetting that iodine is a potent caustic? Is he perhaps forgetting that cauterized tissue does not bleed? And how does he explain that Padre Pio's wounds, though daubed with iodine or tincture of iodine, are always bleeding and with sparkling blood? And if the wounds are superficial, why is it that in cauterizing them, the tincture of iodine does not prevent the flow of blood?...
>
> Scientifically, wounds will heal if they are well cared for, or they will have complications if they are neglected.
>
> Now, is it possible to explain scientifically why Padre Pio's wounds, not treated in accordance with any scientific procedure, washed (especially his hands) in anything but sterile water, covered with ordinary woolen gloves or with handkerchiefs taken from the drawer without any disinfectant, or washed with that lowest grade soap, still don't become worse, they don't fester, they don't become infected and neither do they heal? And why have they not healed even after the excellent remedies prescribed by the professor and faithfully used?

These are the judgments of representatives of the world of medical science who were able to observe Padre Pio numerous times. Unfortunately, there were also some among them who either lacked scientific competence or would not even see him.

18

A VISIT NEVER MADE

*I*N THE CHURCH AND MONASTERY OF THE Capuchins at San Giovanni Rotondo, in addition to the regular faithful, ecclesiastical personages also began to visit; for example, His Excellency Alberto Costa, Bishop of Melfi-Rapolla, in August, 1919, who said afterwards that he felt that he had conversed with a saint; and His Excellency Anselmo Kenealy, Archbishop of Simla, on March 24, 1920, who spent five hours in conversation with Padre Pio and knelt before him and asked for his blessing.

Someone thought of providing a guest book that visitors could sign and jot down their thoughts. In this book Padre Agostino Gemelli, O.F.M., founder of Sacred Heart University at Milan, wrote this message on April 18, 1920: "Every day we note that the Franciscan tree is producing more fruit and this is the greatest consolation for anyone who receives nourishment and life from this marvelous tree."

According to the testimony of the former provincial, Padre Benedetto, Gemelli had written for permission to visit Padre Pio. The new provincial, Padre Pietro, responded that if he wanted to do so as a scientist [Padre Gemelli was a medical doctor and psychologist as well as a priest], he would have to have authorization from the ecclesiastical authorities in Rome.

One should also take into consideration the great reluctance of Padre Pio to submit to such examinations and interviews.

Padre Gemelli assured the provincial that it was simply a private visit for spiritual reasons. But when he arrived at San Giovanni Rotondo with Armida Barelli, his collaborator, the vicar general of the diocese, the bishop's secretary and the Lenten preacher from the cathedral, he wanted to examine the stigmata of Padre Pio. It was Armida Barelli who first asked that Padre Gemelli be allowed to examine the wounds, but Padre Benedetto had to insist that permission had not been granted for that. Then Padre Gemelli asked if he could have a private conversation with Padre Pio. They spoke for a few minutes in the sacristy, and Padre Gemelli told Padre Pio that he wanted to make a clinical examination of the wounds. Padre Pio told him that unless the ecclesiastical authorities had given permission in writing, he would have to politely but firmly refuse. Padre Pio than headed for the church to celebrate Mass.

Although Padre Gemelli made the same request many times, he not only did not succeed in making a clinical examination, but he never even saw the wounds of the saintly Capuchin friar. Nevertheless, the word started to circulate that the famous Padre Gemelli had examined the wounds and had submitted a very negative report to the ecclesiastical authorities. Then, in 1924, on the occasion of the seventh centenary of the stigmata of St. Francis of Assisi, Padre Gemelli published an article under the title *Le affermazioni della scienza sulla stigmate di san Francesco* (Affirmations of Science Regarding the Stigmata of St. Francis) in which he asserted that the only authentic stigmata of supernatural origin was the one received by St. Francis and, with some reserve, that of St. Catherine of Siena. For all the others, he declared that "the diagnosis of hysteria has a reasonable foundation." They are induced artificially, although unconsciously. Thus, with one stroke, Padre Gemelli rejected the stigmata of Padre Pio and all others, some of whom have been raised to the honor of the altar. This led to a great deal of polemics.

The Italian magazine, *La Civiltà Cattolica,* branded these statements as "inexact and imprudent." Also, the theory adopted by Gemelli that even in regard to the stigmata of St. Francis of Assisi, the wounds were the result of new formations of skin, was severely criticized. Doctor Festa also reacted vehemently against the opinions of Padre Gemelli and he demonstrated scientifically that Padre Pio, "signed by the sacred marks of the stigmata, was not hysterical nor a psychopath, and not a pretender or a victim of self-inflicted wounds."

Meanwhile, the name and the person of Padre Pio were the objects of superficial judgments, incredulity and skepticism. Faith, fanaticism and calumny were all intermingled, and the press printed everything and anything that would feed the flames of sensationalism.

Padre Pio listened, read, suffered and prayed. He kept himself aloof from disputes and discussions. He kept in mind always the command that the Lord had given him: "Sanctify yourself and sanctify others." That was his mission.

He fixed his gaze resolutely on the cross and in that sign he saw the universal dimensions of his love: the vertical dimension of the love of God and the horizontal dimension of the love of neighbor. His love of his brethren burned brightly within him. These two dimensions were the scope of his spirituality.

19

CHURCH AUTHORITIES
INTERVENE

*M*EN DO NOT LIGHT A LAMP AND THEN put it under a bushel basket. They set it on a stand where it gives light to all in the house" (Mt 5:15). And at San Giovanni Rotondo a bright light was shining, illumined by God's grace and resplendent before men, thus giving glory to God. Unbelievers were converted; the lukewarm were filled with fervor; those who practiced virtue made great progress on the road to perfection. Everyone wanted to speak with the friar with the stigmata; everyone wanted to touch him. The church was always filled, and in a short time the Capuchin monastery lost its customary quiet and tranquillity. Day after day the crowds grew larger. Immersed in an intense priestly ministry, Padre Pio wrote on June 3, 1919:

> I don't have a minute of free time; it is all releasing brethren from the grip of Satan. Blessed be God! The greatest charity is that of liberating souls captivated by Satan and winning them for Christ. This is what I do assiduously, night and day. Countless persons from all classes and of both sexes come here for the single purpose of going to confession, and I am called upon for that. There are marvelous conversions (*Epistolario*, I, 1145s).

In the hours of the night Padre Pio dedicated himself to the delicate and demanding task of spiritual direction by letters. By this time there were numerous persons under his spiritual care, seeking to be enriched by his teaching and to receive encouragement and new motivation for living out their vocation to holiness. His letters emanated an indefinable warmth which stimulated the readers to travel along the path to holiness by the way of asceticism. He constantly urged them to try to discern God's will for them and to follow it generously.

During the day he rescued souls from Satan's grasp by administering the sacrament of reconciliation. For some time now he had the faculties to hear the confessions of both men and women, but he would hear only men's confessions in the sacristy. The fame of the Capuchin friar was spreading everywhere. Even the Cardinal Secretary of State, Pietro Gasparri, wrote to the Capuchin superior on November 19, 1919, to recommend the Rosi family, who wanted to confess and receive Communion from Padre Pio, and also to ask him to pray for the Pope's intentions and for his own. He also asked for some little object from the Padre for his niece Antonia Veda.

Yet the Capuchin friars never did anything to advertise the phenomena surrounding Padre Pio, and they deplored the publicity made by the press and forbidden by canon law. The *carabinieri* of the region sometimes had to intervene to keep order among the pilgrims. The prefect of Foggia wrote a letter to the central office for security on June 28, 1919, stating that there would be a serious problem for public order if the Church authorities ever tried to move Padre Pio. Evidently, the prospect had already been mentioned in high places.

As a matter of fact, the rumor spread throughout the region in September that Padre Pio was going to be transferred soon. The faithful and the citizens in general expressed their disappointment by massive public demonstrations. Padre Egidio announced from the altar that they should not believe the rumor about Padre Pio's imminent transfer and that they should all stay calm. Nevertheless, many people didn't trust him, and they stayed around to guard the monastery until after midnight.

In the summer of 1920 the rumor began to circulate again with even greater insistence and it caused a veritable revolution among the citizens. So much so that it triggered the beginning of a series of apostolic visitations by Archbishop Bonaventura Cerretti, Secretary for Extraordinary Ecclesiastical Affairs, on May 29, 1920. He wrote in the guest book an expression of thanks for the cordial and truly Franciscan reception given him and he asked the prayers of Padre Pio. On the following July 12, Padre Luigi Besi, Postulator General of the Passionists, also made an apostolic visitation and wrote that Padre Pio "was privileged by God, as was St. Gemma, but even more so."

Padre Besi had been struck by an element of the extraordinary even before he met Padre Pio. Without anyone having any knowledge whatever of his mission, on his arrival he found a gentleman awaiting him with a carriage to take him to the friary. Later he learned that Padre Pio had told the superior: "Send the carriage to the station, because a Passionist Father is arriving, sent by the Pope personally."

The people meanwhile were constantly on guard. On June 25, 1921, a visiting priest was suspected by the people as the one assigned to prepare for the transfer of Padre Pio, and they stormed the monastery. Four months later, Cardinal Agosto Silj, accompanied by Bishop Giuseppe De Angelis, arrived at San Giovanni Rotondo. He had a meeting with Padre Pio and was satisfied with everything. It is certain that the Cardinal made a detailed report to Pope Benedict XV, who also expressed a favorable opinion. In fact, in a private audience granted to Bishop Fernando Damiani of Uruguay, he said: "Truly, Padre Pio is one of those extraordinary men whom God sends to earth from time to time for the conversion of souls."

On other occasions also Pope Benedict XV expressed his favorable opinion of Padre Pio. For example, he once said to the lawyer, Cesare Festa, who had been converted from Masonry by the Capuchin friar: "Oh yes, Padre Pio is truly a man of God;

no one ever doubted that, but you can help to make it known." And to a consultor to the Holy Office he once said: "I am convinced that Padre Pio brings souls to the Lord. As long as this is his mission, my mission is to remain at his side."

However, the echo of events at San Giovanni Rotondo attracted the attention of the Holy Office, and on May 10, 1922, it issued its own decree. With this precautionary document, approved by Pope Pius XI, the Holy Office commanded that every singularity and rumor about Padre Pio should be avoided; that in all respects he was to follow the practices of the common life; he was not to celebrate Mass at a fixed hour, but on a variable schedule, preferably early in the morning and in private; under no conditions was he to show or let people kiss his hands.

Moreover, the Holy Office stated that by his words and actions Padre Pio was to make known to his confreres and to people outside, his firm will to be left alone so that he could attend to his own sanctification. Furthermore, he should have a different spiritual director than Padre Benedetto, with whom every form of communication, even by letter, must be terminated.

Finally, to guarantee the exact fulfillment of the decree, the Holy Office commanded that Padre Pio should be moved out of San Giovanni Rotondo, far from his Capuchin province, for example, to northern Italy. Nevertheless, because there could be some difficulty at the local level, for now, only the preparations should be made so that the transfer could be effected as soon as it was possible. Last of all, Padre Pio was forbidden to respond to any letters asking for his advice, graces or prayers.

When Padre Pio was informed of the regulations that applied to him, he bowed his head and obeyed. Padre Benedetto did the same, and for twenty years, until his death, he cut off all relations with his beloved spiritual son.

The provincial, Padre Pietro, sent a letter to the Minister General of the Order on July 28, 1922, to assure him that the regulations issued by the Holy Office were being carried out in the best way possible. For some time now there had been a constant and strict vigilance over Padre Pio and those around him.

By reason of his character and temperament, Padre Pio already shunned any kind of singularity and in all things he observed the common life, except as regards the refectory, since by reason of poor health, he was given only that food — which in no sense could be considered delicacies — that his stomach will retain.

Padre Pietro also explained that the late hour assigned to Padre Pio for the celebration of Mass was chosen for the convenience of persons who come from a distance, so that the confreres assigned to teaching can be free, and to give Padre Pio the time to go to confession before celebrating Mass. Then the provincial added:

> It would not be easy for Padre Pio to show his hands or allow them to be kissed, because they are always covered with gloves, and during the celebration of Mass he does his best to hide them in his sleeves. I am not aware that he has ever spoken to anyone about his wounds. I myself have witnessed the repugnance — I would even say pain — that he suffers when obliged to show them during medical examination.

As regards letter-writing, the provincial said that letters containing requests for advice and counsel were handled by a prudent confessor, and those requesting favors were answered with the promise of prayers.

Consequently, the major problem had to do with the transfer of Padre Pio. Padre Pietro stated that he had thought about that possibility since the beginning of his term as provincial, but the repeated demonstrations by the people of San Giovanni Rotondo caused him to put it aside. Also the civil prefect of Foggia, who was responsible for whatever happened after an attempt to transfer Padre Pio, dissuaded him from taking that action.

Nevertheless, in spite of this clarification and the detailed report, the affair gained momentum. The official bulletin of the Vatican published a document issued by the Holy Office and dated May 31, 1923, which declared that after an investigation of the phenomena attributed to Padre Pio, they did not appear to be supernatural in origin. Therefore, the faithful were to adapt their behavior to this declaration.

The people of San Giovanni Rotondo rose up in protest. On June 25 there was a public demonstration against any change made concerning Padre Pio. The citizens also sent a telegram to the provincial, saying that in the name of justice they would not permit the removal of Padre Pio from San Giovanni Rotondo. The superior of the Capuchin community, Padre Ignazio, reported as follows to the provincial:

> A large crowd of three thousand people, accompanied by music and civil and military authorities, marched up to the monastery and demanded assurances that Padre Pio would not be removed and that he could celebrate public Masses. The mayor and other civil authorities came into the monastery to persuade me to suspend the application of the restrictions.

Meanwhile, the provincial had received from the civil prefect at Foggia a request that Padre Pio be permitted to celebrate Mass in front of the people, "in order not to cause new disturbances of public order." So the provincial was caught between the obligation to enforce the restrictions and the impossibility of controlling the reaction of the people, who were disposed to resort to violence if necessary. He explained his delicate position to his superiors, and on June 26, 1923, they granted permission for Padre Pio to celebrate Mass in the church, "to avoid grave inconveniences and to pacify the excitement of the people."

Meanwhile, the Holy Office was asking clarification as to how the regulations given to the Procurator General of the Capuchins were being carried out. In order to have the latest precise information, Padre Melchiorre sent a request to the provincial, Padre Pietro. But the provincial was sick at the time, so Padre Luigi, the vicar provincial, even though "fearing serious consequences," sent the reply, and assured Padre Melchiorre that he would see to the transfer of Padre Pio from San Giovanni Rotondo promptly and prudently.

Consequently, on July 31, the Minister General of the Capuchins summoned Padre Luigi to Rome and gave him the "obedience" for Padre Pio. He then wrote two letters. One was to the Holy Office, stating that he had given orders to the vicar provincial, Padre Luigi, to effect the transfer, but to do so with prudence and firmness, not to be afraid of any difficulties, but to use every means to see that Padre Pio was transferred. The second letter was addressed to the provincial of Picena, stating that Padre Pio had been assigned to the friary in Ancona.

Six days later, the provincial at Foggia was advised by his superior in Rome to seek the intervention of the civil authorities and the cooperation of Padre Pio to facilitate the transfer. Then, in the early days of August, Padre Luigi went to San Giovanni Rotondo to inform Padre Pio about the "obedience" from the Minister General. Late in the evening he called Padre Pio to his room, read the "obedience" to him and asked him to be ready to leave.

Later on, Padre Luigi stated that Padre Pio bowed his head and with folded arms responded: "At your service; let's leave at once. When I am with the superior, I am with God."

Padre Luigi asked him: "But do you want to leave with me at once? It's late at night. Where shall we go?"

"I don't know," answered Padre Pio. "I will go with you when and where you wish."

But it was midnight! Controlling his emotions, Padre Luigi said: "I have orders only to communicate to you the obedience; it will be executed only when I receive further instructions from Rome."

When he heard the news, Francesco Morcaldi, the mayor of San Giovanni Rotondo went to see the prefect at Foggia, who listened to the news and then commented that "the transfer is feasible but it's not possible to avoid bloodshed."

The mayor returned to San Giovanni Rotondo and went to see Padre Pio. "Padre," he asked, "are you going?"

The Capuchin responded: "If that is the order, I cannot do other than obey the will of my superiors. I am a son of obedience."

The two men embraced and wept.

The people, however, could not accept the idea of losing Padre Pio. They constructed barricades along the streets leading to the monastery and, armed with sticks, guns and clubs, they were ready for anything. They even took turns at surveillance.

On August 10, after Vespers, a bricklayer from the neighboring village of San Marco approached Padre Pio, and pointing his pistol at him, he said: "Living or dead, you will stay here with us!" Fortunately, some men rushed him and immobilized him. Two days later, Padre Pio wrote to Mayor Morcaldi:

> The events of the past few days have profoundly troubled me and they worry me a great deal, because they make me fear that involuntarily I may be the cause of violent happenings in this my beloved city. I pray to God that he will prevent such a catastrophe, letting any suffering fall on me.
>
> But if, as you say, my transfer is already decided, I pray you to bring it about by every means so that the will of my superiors, which is the will of God, may be carried out, for I must obey it blindly.
>
> I shall always remember this generous people in my poor prayers, asking peace and prosperity for them, and as a token of my love for them, since I can do nothing else, I express my desire that if my superiors do not oppose it, my bones will rest in some quiet corner of this soil.
>
> Respectfully yours in the sweet Lord (*Epistolario,* IV, 734).

Meanwhile, the head of the Italian police, General Emilio De Bono, commissioned one of his functionaries, Carmelo Camilleri, to investigate the situation at San Giovanni Rotondo and submit a report. When Camilleri arrived at the friary, he heard Padre Pio ask: "Have you come to take me away? I am at your disposition, but I ask you to act prudently; not for me, but because I do not want any harm done to these poor people who are trying to defend my residence in this place."

The police official was astonished at the intuition of Padre Pio. He made his investigation and gathered testimony worthy of belief. He then returned to Rome and made his report to General De Bono, adding that to take Padre Pio away from the monastery at San Giovanni Rotondo, it would be necessary to use force, and there would be bloodshed. The General understood clearly the state of affairs and going through the proper channels, he began immediately to work for the revocation of the order issued by the ecclesiastical authorities. The end result was that the transfer of Padre Pio was suspended.

On April 20, 1924, another apostolic visitor arrived at the friary in San Giovanni Rotondo. He was Padre Celestino of Desio, who had come seeking information about some things pertaining to the community, the crowds of visitors, Padre Pio's manner of celebrating Mass, and the persons who attended his Mass. On July 24 of that same year there was a third intervention by the Holy Office, prompted by new sources of information, in order to curb the increasing fanaticism and to exhort the faithful to refrain from visiting Padre Pio and from any kind of contact with him, even by letter.

In silence, Padre Pio prayed and offered to God the bitter chalice of his suffering. He plumbed the very depths of sorrow and discovered its salvific meaning and precious fruit. Suffering is what in fact purified, converted and gave proof of his love for God and it was also beneficial for the salvation of souls.

20

SACRIFICES SUFFERED AND OFFERED

$\mathcal{A}$T THE END OF SEPTEMBER IN 1925, Doctor Giorgio Festa, seeking some quiet and repose, decided to return once again to the friary at San Giovanni Rotondo. It was more than five years since he had examined the wounds of Padre Pio. He arrived at the friary just as it was getting dark and the friars welcomed him, happy to have him as their guest. They assigned a small guest room to him.

A few days later, Doctor Festa engaged Padre Pio in cordial conversation which was suddenly interrupted. Padre Pio's face was contorted in an expression of pain. Doctor Festa asked him at once what could have caused that unexpected change of countenance.

"For some years," said Padre Pio, "I have had a sharp pain in my stomach. When I ascend the steps of the altar I sometimes have shooting pains. Do me a favor; examine me and give me a remedy that will enable me to do my duty."

With the affection and delicacy of a son, the doctor began the examination and he noticed a large hernia on his left side. He noted that it was irreducible because of extensive adhesions. The examination further revealed that the area was extremely sensitive to pain. It required surgery, and right away.

"Tell the superior," said Padre Pio, "and if he has no objections, you can operate on me."

Doctor Festa was somewhat hesitant and uncertain. He felt the weight of a very particular responsibility and he asked Padre Pio to pray to the Lord in order to find out if he is the one who should perform the operation.

Padre Pio replied: "No; I won't make that prayer. It would offend God. Hasn't Jesus taught that we should love one another and do good to one another? If this happens, he blesses our actions. So why do you make it necessary for him to repeat it? The Lord will surely bless and guide your hand because you are doing a good deed."

Admiring such great faith, Doctor Festa spoke with the superior and scheduled the operation for October 5, 1925. The doctor needed surgical instruments, so he sent Giuseppe De Paoli, who frequently visited the friary, to fetch them at his office in Rome. Some time previously the superior had arranged to have the wall between two rooms removed in order to provide a large recreation room that the students could use during the long winter days. On seeing that it was large and freshly painted, Doctor Festa decided that it would serve well as an operating room. A large table was put in place for the patient and a smaller table was set up on which to place the instruments and other necessary equipment.

Doctor Festa asked his colleague, Doctor Angelo Merla, to be his assistant. Padre Fortunato, who had served in a military hospital during the war, was chosen to be the nurse.

At nine o'clock in the morning on October 5, Giuseppe De Paoli arrived from Rome with the surgical instruments, gauze and anaesthetic. All the instruments were immediately sterilized. After celebrating Mass and hearing some confessions, Padre Pio arrived, but it was already 11:45. His face showed signs of weariness and ill-concealed suffering. He took off his habit and put on a white hospital gown. He then said: "Doctor, I put myself in your hands. But I want to tell you that I do not want to be put under an anaesthetic." The doctor was amazed at this and he tried to talk the Padre out of it. But it was useless! Padre Pio assured him that he would not move during the surgery.

Doctor Festa was thinking that perhaps Padre Pio was unwilling to be anaesthetized because he feared that strangers might be curious to examine his stigmata. Doctor Festa, of course, had already observed and even studied them.

Padre Pio placed a relic of the true Cross on a small table and asked that a candle be lighted on either side of the reliquary. Then he joked with Doctor Leandro Giuva, who had arrived unexpectedly. Padre Pio knew that the doctor also had a hernia, so he told him that it would be his turn next and to be ready for surgery "while the instruments were still warm." He then stretched himself out on the makeshift operating table and placed his hands behind his head.

Doctor Festa began by injecting five shots of local anaesthetic, just as the church bell began to ring at twelve o'clock and Padre Pio started to recite the *Angelus*. As the surgery progressed and the doctor had to cut more deeply into the tissue and muscle, the pain likewise increased. The suffering must have been intense. Now and then Padre Pio groaned and Doctor Festa marvelled at his voluntary suffering heroically endured.

After about an hour, the eyes of Padre Pio were brimming over and the tear drops rolled down his cheeks. Then his lips moved and he said: "Hurry, please! I cannot stand any more!" Then, after a brief pause, he prayed: "Pardon me, Jesus, if I don't know how to suffer as I ought."

The surgeon was deeply moved and he hastened as best he could to finish the operation which, at that point, must have been terribly painful. By this time Padre Pio was praying: "My Lord, my God, pardon me! What a shame! I have never been able to offer you anything in my life and now, with this little that I suffer, with this trifle in comparison with your Passion, I groan, I give up!" Then he collapsed. His pulse was very weak. He had passed out.

At that moment Doctor Festa took the opportunity to check the wound in Padre Pio's side. It looked fresh and bright red, as he had seen it five years before. Emanating from its contours were what looked like rays of light.

Doctor Festa then attended to the closing of the surgery and the stitches. As he was finishing, Padre Pio came to and was told that it was all finished. With a smile, he turned to Doctor Leandro Giuva: "Leandrino! Leandrino! It's your turn!"

It was two o'clock in the afternoon. A few friars carried Padre Pio to his cell. Talking among themselves later, they concluded that Padre Pio had refused the anaesthesia because the superiors had forbidden him to let anyone see the stigmata. But Padre Ignazio stated categorically that it was because Padre Pio wanted to be conscious so he could know what was happening to him. There were few who thought that Padre Pio was simply offering himself to suffer. Padre Pio himself had said to a friend on that very afternoon, in the midst of the pain he was suffering: "Do you think that the Lord has accepted my sacrifice for the health of…?"

"Oh Father," his friend replied, "when has the Lord not accepted your sacrifices?"

Padre Pio commented: "You are not a good judge!"

Until late in the evening he mentally reviewed all the steps of the surgery. He saw again the relic of the true Cross between the two lighted candles and he fingered the beads of his rosary.

Two years later, Doctor Festa had to operate on Padre Pio again. He had been advised by friends and colleagues in San Giovanni Rotondo that the Capuchin was suffering from a cyst or tumor on his neck. He arranged to see Padre Pio in the middle of September, 1927, and after examining the patient, he scheduled surgery for the following day.

This time also, Padre Pio did not want any anaesthesia. Knowing him as well as he did, Doctor Festa did not insist. Aided once again by his colleague, Doctor Angelo Merla, he removed the cyst, which was about as big as a pigeon's egg.

During the operation, which took about half an hour, Padre Pio did not react in any way whatever.

"Padre," asked the doctor, "didn't you feel any pain?"

"Of course I did," he responded.

"Then why no movement of the head, no sound?"

"And why should I have moved my head or cried out?" said Padre Pio. "I would have embarrassed you, and as a result, your work would have taken longer, and also my pain. So you see, by not making a sound, I have acted only in my own interest."

Those words, stated with an ironic smile, concealed another offering made to the Lord for the salvation of a soul or its healing.

21

AN INSUPPORTABLE GRIEF

*D*URING THE YEARS 1927 AND 1928 TWO more apostolic visitators were sent to San Giovanni Rotondo: Bishop Felice Bevilacqua, who stayed at the friary from March 26 to April 5, and Bishop Giuseppe Bruno, from the Sacred Congregation of the Council. The sufferings of Padre Pio had been increasing, but in the early days of 1929 he suffered a sorrow that was truly insupportable: the loss of his beloved mother.

Ever since her son had returned to San Giovanni Rotondo to remain permanently in the cloister, Giuseppa had kept to herself in Pietrelcina. She kept her distance from the events that were occurring around her Francesco, getting information from friends and relatives. Her heart always trembled with fear and anxiety.

On December 5, 1928, she was invited by Mary Adelia Pyle, a spiritual daughter of Padre Pio whom everybody called *Maria l'americana*, to spend Christmas at San Giovanni Rotondo. Delighted at the opportunity to be a little closer to her son, Mamma Peppa accepted the invitation and was a guest at Mary's home, which was very close to the friary. Her meeting with Padre Pio took place in the square in front of the church. This is the way Mary Pyle described it:

Hiding her great joy under an apparent calm, Peppa took the hand of her son and before he could pull away, she said: "Padre Pio, I kiss your hand for Aunt Libera (first kiss) and for Aunt Pellegrina (second kiss), for Aunt Filomena (third kiss)," and so on, until she had kissed his hand ten times for aunts and godmothers. Then she ended by saying: "And now, Padre Pio, I kiss your hand for me." She tried to do so but did not succeed, because as she bent to kiss his hand, Padre Pio suddenly lifted his hands in the air and, holding them aloft, he said: "Never! The son should kiss the hand of the mamma, not the mamma the hand of the son!"

After that, Mamma Peppa did not try to kiss Padre Pio's hand, but every morning after receiving Communion from his hand, without letting anyone see her, she bent down and kissed the ground where the wounded feet of her son had stood.

She was confused by the things she heard about him. She wished to do something, but she was not allowed to do anything. When she saw the superior, Padre Raffaele, in the sacristy, she approached him and in all simplicity she said: "Father Guardian, love my son Padre Pio!"

Padre Raffaele, deeply moved by that "recommendation," which was an expression of all the love and tenderness of a mother, responded: "Mamma Peppa, don't worry; don't be afraid. But take care of yourself because it is very cold."

Actually, she was wearing clothes that were too light for that season of the year. She had refused a heavier garment that Mary Pyle had offered her because she felt it was more proper for a great lady.

After attending the Mass celebrated by Padre Pio on Christmas Eve, she returned home shivering. They put her to bed and took her temperature. It was very high! The next day the doctor made an examination and diagnosis: double pneumonia!

Accompanied by Padre Raffaele, Padre Pio went to see his mother several times. When he saw that she was at the end of her life, he administered the sacrament of the sick and remained at her bedside. When he saw that she would soon draw her last breath, he could not remain any longer. He kissed her on the forehead, uttered a loud sob and left. He had to be led away by two doctors.

Padre Raffaele took his place at the bedside and the humble woman breathed her last and returned her soul to God. It was 6:15 in the afternoon on January 3, 1929.

In a neighboring room, Padre Pio abandoned himself to uncontrolled heart-rending weeping. His tears caused all the others to weep as well. He soaked a pile of handkerchiefs with his tears and keep repeating: *"Mamma mia! Mamma mia bella! Mamma mia!"*

One of his spiritual sons, in an effort to comfort him, said: "Padre, you taught us that sorrow is nothing else but an expression of the love offered to God. So why do you weep like this?"

He answered: "But these are precisely tears of love. Nothing but love."

Countless people wanted to pray at the mortal remains of Mamma Peppa, dressed in the habit of a Franciscan tertiary. The funeral on the following day was impressive. Sorrow had physically prostrated Padre Pio, and at the advice of the doctors, he remained in the home of Mary Pyle for several days. But his confreres did not leave him alone; they took turns staying with him. At night Padre Raffaele slept in a bed that had been put up in the same room.

22

YET ANOTHER TRIAL

*I*N A LETTER WRITTEN TO PADRE AGOSTI-
no on February 13, 1913, Padre Pio had stated that "the most
sweet Jesus" had told him in a spiritual locution:

> Do not be afraid; I will make you suffer, but I will also
> give you strength. I desire that your soul, by a daily and
> hidden martyrdom, should be purified and tested. Do
> not be surprised if I permit the devil to tempt you, the
> world to disgust you, persons dearest to you to afflict
> you, because nothing can prevail against those who
> mourn beneath the cross for love of me and whom I exert
> myself to protect (*Epistolario*, I, 339).

Faithful to his prediction, the Lord now wanted to test the
faith, hope and love of Padre Pio. He wanted to try his fortitude,
patience, obedience, and all his other virtues.

On March 31, 1931, the provincial summoned Padre Raffaele to Foggia to inform him confidentially that the Capuchin
superiors in Rome would be sending a new Father Guardian
from Milan to the friary at San Giovanni Rotondo. When Padre
Raffaele returned to San Giovanni Rotondo, he discovered that
some lay persons were already aware of the news and were
spreading it around. Once the mayor of San Giovanni Rotondo

got wind of it, he considered it his duty to speak openly about it, because he felt that it was his obligation to defend Padre Pio. The people of the place got together and took the initiative as soon as they heard that an "outsider" had arrived at the friary. The person referred to was Padre Eugenio Tignola, a Friar Minor who was passing through and had asked for hospitality.

During the night, between April 6 and 7, a crowd of about 100 people assembled in the square in front of the church. Most of them were armed to the teeth. They forced the front door of the friary and entered the cloister. They demanded that the Friar Minor who, so they thought, was "the new superior from Milan," should be turned over to them so they could send him back.

The superior sent for Padre Pio, in the hope that at least he would be able to restore peace and calm. Padre Pio was in his cell, so he came to the window next to the choir and assured the people that the "stranger" was only a temporary guest at the friary. But the people would not believe him, because they thought that he spoke that way only out of obedience to Padre Raffaele. In the end the mayor and the *carabinieri*, who were ready to keep vigil all night long if necessary, finally convinced the demonstrators to go home.

The superior wrote to the provincial and told him that at the present time it was impossible to go forward. Then, in the name of the whole community, he denounced the "hostile demonstration by ill-intentioned" people who, he claimed, had thrown stones at the windows, forced their way through the door and violated the cloister.

The provincial reported the incident to the Minister General of the Order, who asked for further detailed, confidential information. He was told that the people of the region did not want the religious community to be governed by a superior from outside because in their minds this represented the first step towards the transfer of Padre Pio to a distant monastery. Consequently, the situation was serious and the monastery was being watched day and night by people who were ready for anything.

On the evening of June 9 the superior at San Giovanni Rotondo was notified of a decree issued by the Holy Office on May 23, 1931, containing a serious provision. Padre Pio was deprived of all the faculties for priestly ministry, except the celebration of Mass, which, however, was to be done not in the church but privately, in a chapel inside the cloister and without anyone else participating.

As soon as he read the decree, Padre Raffaele was overcome with a feeling of perplexity and discomfort. On the morning of June 10 he went to consult the provincial at Foggia. There was nothing anyone could do. The decree must be carried out immediately!

Returning to San Giovanni Rotondo, Padre Raffaele first spoke with the friars. Then, after Vespers, he summoned Padre Pio and told him the content of the decree. He was not to celebrate public Masses nor hear the confessions of the laity or the friars. Padre Pio simply raised his eyes to heaven and said: "God's will be done!" Then he covered his face with his hands, bowed his head and did not say another word.

Padre Raffaele tried to comfort him but he sought comfort only in Jesus hanging on the cross, because a little later he went to the choir and stayed there until after midnight. The following day was the feast of *Corpus Christi* and he celebrated Mass in an internal chapel of the friary. He spent three hours in prayer and in the celebration of the Mass. He did the same on the following days.

Padre Pio suffered terribly because he was no longer able to "snatch souls from Satan's power and lead them to God." The press promptly spread the news and the restrictions provoked great displeasure everywhere as well as lively protests and indignation. The *carabinieri* at San Giovanni Rotondo were ready again to check any outbreaks or demonstrations. Padre Raffaele described the situation in a letter to the Minister General of the Capuchins on June 17.

On the evening of June 11, a group of people gathered together in the friary with the intention of staging a demonstration, but at the right moment the *carabinieri* intervened and politely convinced the people to disperse and go home. They did the same thing on a few other evenings during the week.

The discontent of the people is constantly increasing. Actually, there is relative calm externally because everyone hopes that the restrictions will be lifted in a peaceful manner..., but with the passing of time, this hope will vanish, and I can't say how they will then proceed to end the affair.

As we can well imagine, the superior was going through some very difficult days. Padre Pio suffered and prayed as well, but he always remained calm, serene and tranquil. Completely submissive to the will of God, he endured it all for the love of God and the good of souls.

His spiritual sons and daughters prayed with him and for him at a distance. One of them openly criticized the procedure that had made Padre Pio a veritable exile and recluse. Years later, after admitting his criticism, Padre Pio told him: "You did wrong. We must respect the decrees of the Church. If the Holy Office saw fit to issue that decree, it did so to avoid fanaticism, and we should suffer in silence."

During those difficult days Padre Agostino also visited Padre Pio, and at the beginning he found him very depressed. He had even wept for a few minutes, but gradually his spirits lifted somewhat. "He was always resigned, however depressed by the new trial."

Padre Pio bore his suffering with fortitude and trust in God. He celebrated Mass in an interior chapel, with the door closed, and then spent at least an hour in thanksgiving. Later he would go to the library to study Sacred Scripture or read the history of the Church or *The Divine Comedy*. The friars noted that he always had the rosary in his hand. Like St. Francis of Assisi, rather than a friar who prays, he had become the very personification of prayer.

Besides being deprived of the presence of Padre Pio, the people of San Giovanni Rotondo were mortified to see on September 28, 1932, the transfer of all the young students for the priesthood. There were complaints and protests which ignited the fires that were still burning beneath the ashes. Numerous people began to lose patience. Days and months passed, but the situation remained unchanged.

On March 14, 1933, it seemed that something was about to happen. Two important personages from Rome appeared at the door of the friary: Bishop Luca Pasetto, of the Congregation for Religious, and Bishop Felice Bevilacqua, who had made a previous apostolic visitation in 1927. Bishop Pasetto was himself a Capuchin and, before lunch, he had a lengthy visit with Padre Pio. Then, in the afternoon, he took a long walk with the superior, Padre Raffaele, on the road leading to the monastery. He told the superior that he had been greatly edified by the humility, docility and comportment of Padre Pio. He saw him as a man of prayer and totally dedicated to God.

This gave Padre Raffaele some reason for hope and it was further augmented when the new archbishop of Manfredonia, Andrea Cesarano, made his first visit to San Giovanni Rotondo on June 23 of that same year. Numerous persons approached the archbishop, asking him to intercede on behalf of Padre Pio. The next day the archbishop himself met Padre Pio and was very cordial and affable to him. There was something new in the air!

Late in the afternoon of July 15, the provincial, Padre Bernardo, returned from a visit to Rome and went directly to San Giovanni Rotondo. First he met with the superior, Padre Raffaele, then, when the community assembled for the evening meal, the provincial sent for Padre Pio who, as usual, was praying in the choir.

"What is it?" he asked the superior.

"We are all suspended *a divinis!*" Padre Raffaele replied, as a joke. He could hardly restrain his happiness, and a few moments later they all entered the refectory.

When they were all seated, the provincial announced: "*Deo gratias!* I have encouraging news to tell you. Padre Pio may again celebrate Mass in the church and hear the confessions of the religious."

Padre Pio was trembling with emotion. He rose from his place, went and knelt before the provincial and kissed his hand, thanking the Holy Father for his goodness. On the next day, July 16, the feast of Our Lady of Mount Carmel, Padre Pio once again celebrated Mass in the public church. The succession of events was described by the provincial in a letter to the procurator general of the Order:

> This letter is to inform you that this past Saturday I left for San Giovanni Rotondo at 13:30 and in the evening, in the refectory, I informed the religious that the supreme authority of the Church, taking into consideration the explanation and the request of our beloved Father General, and aware of the extraordinary Holy Year of the Redemption, granted to our Father General the faculty of permitting Padre Pio of Pietrelcina to celebrate Mass in the church of the friary and authorizing him to hear the confessions of our religious outside the church. I also told them how they should conduct themselves, not speaking of this to anyone. In fact, on Sunday morning, July 16, since the entire matter had been kept secret, there were very few people in the church for the nine-o'clock Mass...
>
> I recommended very strongly the greatest possible composure, order and seriousness, avoiding any unwanted public manifestation in the church or elsewhere. Give some thought to extending the cloister to include the sacristy of the church and taking other opportune precautions...
>
> Thanks be to God, yesterday morning at 9:00 o'clock and this morning at 7:15, Padre Pio celebrated Mass in the church without any public manifestation; *rather, in truly edifying silence.* So I gave the order that Padre Pio should continue to do as he has been doing and make

his preparation and thanksgiving for Mass in the choir. For the time being, Padre Pio only celebrates Mass, and nothing more.

On this past Sunday, July 16, as soon as they knew, all the local authorities came to congratulate him. Then, in the evening, in the hope of seeing Padre Pio again, many people came to the evening services, but Padre Pio remained in choir during the entire function and then retired to his room. And the people went back to their homes without making any kind of disturbance...

In the following days the presence of Padre Pio in the church caused a religious revival among the citizens of San Giovanni Rotondo. Many of them expressed the desire that he be permitted to hear confessions. The provincial made this request of the Minister General and in March, 1934, he granted the faculties for Padre Pio to hear the confessions of men. Then, in May, to hear the confessions of women. After this last trial, Padre Pio resumed his mission for the good of souls, thanks be to God.

23

THE ALTAR
AND THE CONFESSIONAL

$\mathcal{L}$ITTLE BY LITTLE THE CROWDS OF PIL-
grims returned to San Giovanni Rotondo and they kept increasing. Even before sunrise a large number of the faithful would assemble at the door to the church to recite the rosary and the litany of the Blessed Virgin. They would wait for hours, even in the pouring rain or the icy winds of winter, for Padre Pio to celebrate Mass. It was truly a unique and unforgettable experience to assist at his Mass, a tremendous mystery of love and suffering, of pain and blood.

From 2:30 in the morning Padre Pio would be preparing himself for the celebration of Mass. While he was vesting in the sacristy, he would be so absorbed in prayer that it was as if he were not there. At the sound of the little handbell in the hand of the sacristan, he would make his way to the altar. As he walked, he was always bent over as if he were carrying a heavy weight on his shoulders.

"Introibo ad altare Dei..." At those words, all the noise and bustle in the church ceased. At the words *"mea culpa, mea culpa, mea maxima culpa"* of the *Confiteor*, Padre Pio forcefully struck his chest. At that moment it seemed as if he were taking on himself all the sins of mankind. His eyes were closed but they could not hold back his tears.

During the readings his lips moved as if he were "tasting" the word of God as he entered into an intimate colloquium with the heavenly Father. Judging from the nodding of his head and the ecstatic expression on his face, it seemed as if there were an invisible presence that engaged him in a mysterious dialogue.

As the Mass proceeded, Padre Pio gave full expression to his sentiments. Between sobs he pronounced the words of the liturgy. He recommended to God the entire human race, the sick, the poor sinners, his spiritual sons and daughters with their intentions, needs and sorrows. Then, with downcast eyes, he asked their prayers for him in the *Orate fratres*.

Time now is racing by, but Padre Pio is outside time and place. After the hymn of praise at the *Sanctus*, he enters mystically into the various stages of the Passion of Christ: the scourging at the pillar, the crowning with thorns, the crucifixion. When he turns to face the people at the *Dominus vobiscum*, he extends his hands, now free of the gloves that covered his wounds, and the faithful fix their eyes on the wounds of the stigmata. Among the people present, there are murmurings of admiration and devotion.

At the consecration, Padre Pio bows his head towards the host that he holds in his hands and, recalling the events of the Last Supper, he exclaims with loving tenderness: "Jesus, my food!" He hungers and thirsts for the Body and Blood of the Lord, but knowing the weakness of human nature, he repeats in a loud voice: "*Domine, non sum dignus,*" as he forcefully strikes his chest with his right hand. One of the friars expressed his amazement that Padre Pio could clench his fist and strike with such force in spite of the pain of the stigmata. Nevertheless, on receiving the immaculate Body and Blood of Christ, Padre Pio's face is illumined to the point of being transfigured. A profound joy and contentment erase all the signs of pain and suffering. He stands there immobile, with his eyes closed and absorbed in prayer, as if deprived of life. He remains for some time in an ecstasy of love, until he finally turns to the people and dismisses them with *"Ite, missa est."*

The celebration of Mass was not only a visible and tangible sign or expression of his spirituality; it was its very source and origin. For him, the Mass was not simply a celebration of the Eucharistic mystery; it was an active participation in the sacrifice of the Lord. Rarely has the mystery of the Mass become so much a part of the celebrant that he becomes an image of the immolated Christ. One could almost say that it was not that Padre Pio was acting *in persona Christi,* but Jesus was acting *in persona Patris Pii.*

That is why people were drawn to San Giovanni Rotondo from all parts of the world. There the Mass was celebrated by a "living crucifix." On one occasion a spiritual daughter asked Padre Pio what his Mass meant to him, and he answered:

> It is a sacred participation in the passion of Jesus. All that the Lord suffered in his passion, I suffer, to the extent that it is possible to a human being. And that is apart from any merit of mine but entirely due to his goodness. Knowing the passion of Jesus, you will know mine; in the passion of Jesus you will find mine.

All those who attended the Mass celebrated by Padre Pio experienced something of a rebirth to new life. And certainly it gave them a deeper appreciation of the value of the eucharistic sacrifice offered on the altar.

Padre Pio also dedicated himself with particular zeal to the ministry of the confessional. Fifteen, sixteen, at times even nineteen hours a day he spent between the altar and the confessional. His work as an apostle of the confessional was truly admirable. Little by little as his fame spread, a veritable and uncontainable river of humanity flowed into San Giovanni Rotondo. So much so that, to put some discipline into the press of the crowd wanting to go to confession to him, it was found necessary to open an office where one could sign up and take a ticket indicating the order of ingress.

Padre Pio's day began very early. He spent long hours and sometimes whole days in the confessional. Still he never heard a confession on the run. Even the administration of the sacrament of penance meant suffering for him and that is why he has been justly called not only the "apostle" but also the "martyr" of the confessional. He suffered in his own flesh for the sins committed against the Lord. He felt great spiritual sadness at seeing how many of the faithful fail to cooperate with the graces given by God. "They are deaf, blind and insensitive to every sweet invitation and to every reprimand in the name of divine mercy that could move them and convert them. All they do is reinforce their own hardness of heart and intensify their darkness. The thought of seeing so many souls who are determined to remain in their evil in spite of the highest good is an affliction, a torture, a martyrdom for me."

And yet Padre Pio loved these poor sinners, as Jesus loved them. He prostrated himself, he prayed, he stooped to share the moral suffering of the penitent to the point of exhaustion, not only of his physical powers but in a kind of *kenosis* dictated by love, and more particularly in imitation of Christ who, though rich, made himself poor and took upon himself the human condition in all things except sin.

After the periods of time in which he was forbidden to hear confessions, he was anxious to get back to his confessional so that he could "snatch souls from the power of Satan and lead them to God." He was constantly sought after by penitents. Padre Pio not only "confessed" sinners but to a certain extent he became involved in their guilt and repentance. To put it another way, he became a catalyst for them, stimulating their reaction against sin and prompting them to conversion. He did everything possible to facilitate the flow of the grace merited by Christ through the channel of the sacrament of reconciliation. This is the reason for his apparent rudeness or harshness towards penitents who were not sufficiently prepared to receive the sacrament. He insisted that one's confession be brief, clear, integral and sincere. He could not support hesitation, facile justifications or, worse, insincerity. The tone of his voice could at times be severe and harsh.

Actually, he was firm and unyielding with everyone. He did not give sweets to those who needed a purgative. He made no compromises with evil. He hated and condemned sin. And anyone who persisted in sin, he called a devil. This is how he expressed himself to explain his reaction:

> For me, God is always fixed in my mind and stamped on my heart. Never do I lose sight of him. I am able to admire his beauty, his smiles, his affliction, his mercies, his vendettas or, better yet, the rigors of his justice... How is it possible to see God saddened by evil and not be saddened likewise? To see God on the point of discharging his thunder and lightning, and there is no other way of stopping him except to raise one's hand to hold back his arm and to extend the other hand to arouse one's brother, and for a twofold motive: to cast out the evil and get away quickly from that place because the hand of the judge is about to come down on it... For the brethren, how many times, indeed always, I am prompted to say to God the judge in the words of Moses: pardon this people or erase my name from the book of life (*Epistolario*, I, 1247).

Padre Pio never permitted any kind of excuse or extenuating circumstances when it was a question of sin. He intuitively knew immediately if the penitent was truly repentant or only pretending to be so. He had a remarkable ability for penetrating to the interior and reading hearts. He would drive away the hypocrites or the merely curious who approached his confessional simply to have the experience of confessing to him: "Go away and don't come back until..." For some who came to confession without the required disposition, he was known to refuse absolution.

One day one of the friars expressed his disagreement with the way Padre Pio treated some of the penitents in the confessional. His answer was: "If you only knew how I suffer in having to refuse absolution... But remember that it is better to be criticized by man in this life than by God in the next life."

All those who experienced the bitterness of being sent away without absolution, eventually, through the prayers of Padre Pio, were moved to true remorse. They were not at peace! They lived in a state of constant, unbearable agitation which ended only when, after a radical change of life and a total conversion, they turned to the heavenly Father with sincere repentance. Then, their laments of sorrow turned into shouts of joy. When that happened, Padre Pio became infinitely sweet and kind, and solemnly pronounced the longed-for words: *"Ego te absolvo."*

The method of Padre Pio cannot be imitated, and he himself admitted as much when he said to a priest who had dismissed a penitent without absolution: "You cannot do what I do!"

On another occasion he was harsh with a person who had come to him, and the friar who had accompanied the man told him: "But Padre, you've destroyed that soul!"

"No," he replied; "I have pressed him to my heart."

Someone once asked him why he treated his penitents that way. He explained: "I destroy the old and replace it with the new." Another time he said: "Spanking and bread make beautiful children."

Padre Tarcisio remembers that one day, while going up the steps of the friary with Padre Pio, they met a man who asked if he could go to confession. Padre Pio changed his expression and said: "Don't you see how wicked you are? Go and put those things back. Change your life. Then come and I will hear your confession."

Padre Tarcisio was puzzled by Padre Pio's words and after a few steps he said: "Padre, don't be upset!" And Padre Pio replied:

> My son, it is only the external that has assumed a different form. The interior has not changed a bit. And so, before I cause any displeasure to a brother, if you only knew how many arrows have pierced my heart! But if I do not act that way, many souls will not be converted.

Padre Pio knew God with all his attributes and he knew man with all his defects, his weaknesses, his fragility, his miseries and his sins. He loved souls as he loved the Lord. "I am consumed with love of God and love of neighbor," he once wrote. And he felt like a prisoner between these two loves. He was "jealous" of his spiritual sons and daughters. One day he said: "I can punish my spiritual children, but woe to anyone else who touches them! By force of blows I want to carry them upward."

He would remind the penitents of the sins they had committed in the past. He used to say: "I know you inside and out, as you know yourself in the mirror." And if anyone asked him how he could know all that, he would answer: "It is not I but he who is in me and above me."

The sins that upset him the most were the sins against motherhood, the limitation of families, the sins against life, blasphemy and cursing, violation of the Sunday precept, lying, calumny and the scandal of immodest dress.

"Padre," a penitent said to him, "I saw you weeping in the confessional. Why?"

He answered: "Because of the ingratitude of men towards the great divine Benefactor. And what else could Jesus do, that poor Jesus, that he has not done?"

Padre Pio offered himself as a victim for sinners. He would pray and suffer for anyone. He felt within himself a need, an expectation, a hope for God and he was also aware of the needs of men. He always tried to reconcile these two tendencies and he sacrificed himself for the weaker of the two.

"If you only knew what a soul costs!", he once said. And then he added: "Souls are not given as a gift; they must be bought. You don't know what it cost Jesus. And it is always with the same money that it has to be paid for."

While he was hearing confessions, inundated in a sea of corruption, shame and sin, Padre Pio participated in the agony of the Redeemer. There was in him a kind of incarnation of Jesus Christ, as in Jesus Christ there had been an incarnation of God. And all of this not only because of his virtues and charisms, but also because he was a *priest* who regenerated souls through love and suffering; who ransomed souls at the price of his own blood.

In the confessional Padre Pio continued and enlarged his ministry of person-to-person spiritual direction. In the past he had spent long hours at his desk, giving spiritual direction by letter; now, however, a few words usually sufficed. He concentrated on doctrinal instruction and practical advice for living a holy Christian life. In a few cases he dealt with the higher stages of the mystical life, and in these instances he would tell the individuals how to overcome the obstacles and difficulties that one encounters on this higher level. He gave instructions to individuals with a view to helping them realize their full potential. Consequently, he was considered not only a "master of the spiritual life," but a very prudent guide and director. From his manner of speaking and his self-effacing attitude, it was apparent that he had the ability to downplay his role as a mediator, or at least to reduce as much as possible his intervention in the encounter between the divine activity and the soul that had turned to him.

But Padre Pio really was a "mediator." He it was who, without overdoing it or substituting himself for God, led the soul by the hand. He was also a true *prophet*, not in the sense of divinization, but as one who speaks in the name of the Lord, of the Holy Spirit, comforting the soul and bringing it calm, peace and tranquillity; resolving its problems, eliminating difficulties, fulfilling its holy desires and sustaining it in its aspirations. His spiritual direction had only one goal and motivation: the fostering of the interior life and the sanctification of souls, attainable through the working of divine grace and the practice of prayer and intimate union with God.

24

A HOUSE FOR THE SICK

*T*HE OBJECT OF PADRE PIO'S CONCERN was man, the whole man, man composed of body and soul. In attending to the moral misery of his brethren, Padre Pio was not unmindful of their physical weakness, their fragility, their sickness and pain. He was surrounded daily by sick people, by people in need of help, afflicted with every kind of suffering. From his youth he had been acquainted with suffering in its various forms, and for that reason he understood very well the suffering of others. He recognized the hardship for the citizens of San Giovanni Rotondo not to have a hospital. The region was economically depressed, lacking roads and means of communication. The local doctor and his few colleagues were faced daily with a tremendous work load. Frequently they had to perform surgery on their patients in hovels that lacked clean air or sufficient light.

Burning with the fire of charity, Padre Pio had tried as early as 1925 to provide a little hospital for the people of San Giovanni Rotondo. The people had responded enthusiastically to the idea. Thanks to their generous offerings, it was possible to take over a section of the former monastery of the Poor Clares and install the essential medical equipment. The young girls from the Franciscan trade school prepared all the necessary linens and a benefactor in town paid for all the surgical instruments. There were two wards, one for men and one for women, with a total of twenty beds. The Sisters of the Sacred Heart and the Sisters of the Precious Blood were invited to serve as nurses.

The little hospital of St. Francis served the people for thirteen years, but in 1938 an earthquake did irreparable damage and it had to be closed. But the commemorative stone slab was still attached to the facade of the building:

> Padre Pio of Pietrelcina wanted to erect a hospital in this Commune. From among his admirers he collected the funds necessary to complete the work. Doctor Leandro Giuva, president of the Congregation of Charity, overcoming all opposition and obstacles with virile tenacity, made a reality what had been only a dream. Thus, San Giovanni has been gifted with this humanitarian institution. The following are dedicated cooperators: Padre Ignazio, Doctor Antonio Giuva, Angela Serritelli, Secretary Michele Palladino. Members of the Commission: Francesco Morcaldi, Canon Giuseppe Massa, Doctor Angelo Maria Merla, Doctor Alfonso Iodice. January, 1925.

The earthquake of 1938 destroyed everything except Padre Pio's desire and longing to do something to relieve human suffering. In silence, recollection and prayer, he asked the Lord to enlighten him so that he could realize his dream. And the light did come, through the words of his superior, Padre Raffaele, as he was talking one evening about the subject and ended by asking: "Padre Pio, why don't we build a hospital here?" Padre Giocondo and Padre Leone were also present at this conversation.

"And where would we put it?" asked Padre Pio.

"On the land owned by Maria Basilio," said Padre Raffaele.

He was referring to a tract of public land that had been turned over to Maria Basilio by the civil authorities for an institution of charity.

Padre Pio's eyes lit up and he exclaimed: "Let's do it!"

The following day Padre Pio walked out towards the mountain. His stride was uncertain, oscillating, on the uneven ground. After a short distance, he turned back. Now he had a clear idea.

In the square in front of the church he met two of his spiritual daughters, who were watching him with questioning looks. Approaching them, he held out his arms and said: "A great hospital will be built here. Pray with me, my daughters!"

"But Padre," said one of the women, "there is a mountain here!"

"And we shall level the mountain," he replied; and he went back into the church.

Then Padre Pio began to speak about the project to the friends who visited him. Doctor Marco Sanvico, a veterinarian who owned a small industry in Perugia, asked for details. He became enthusiastic about the project and, together with his wife Maria Antonietta, arranged a meeting for January 9, 1940, with Doctor Guglielmo Sanguinetti, who was practicing medicine in Florence, Ida Seitz, Doctor Carlo Kisvarday and his wife Mary. Padre Pio explained his idea to the group and he suggested that a committee be formed for the construction at San Giovanni Rotondo of a hospital in accordance with the intention of the founder, who for the present did not want to be named.

All in the group were in agreement. At the end of the meeting, the men gathered in Padre Pio's cell to review the results of the discussion. Then Padre Pio rose and in a solemn tone he said: "This evening has seen the beginning of my work on earth. I bless all of you and all who will contribute to the work, which will be very great and very beautiful." Then he added: "I wish to make the first donation." He reached into his pocket and drew out a coin, a twenty-franc gold piece which a woman had given him that day. The others followed his example and the subscription list was started.

On January 14, responding to the question submitted by Doctor Sanvico, Padre Pio stated that the project would be called *Casa Sollievo della Sofferenza* (House for the Relief of Suffering). Padre Pio's original plan was to care for the sick and suffering, not in a hospital, clinic or institution, but in a house in which they could obtain relief from their sickness and from their moral and physical sufferings.

The members of the committee advertised the project in a six-page pamphlet printed at Perugia. They described it as a huge hospital to be constructed at San Giovanni Rotondo, which would be "an expression of the charity of Christ which could treat any sick person free of charge." They added the following details:

> Numerous times we have heard from the lips and priestly heart of the Padre this ardent desire. Trusting in divine Providence, we have decided to make it a reality.
>
> This will be a way of demonstrating to God our gratitude for the graces received in this rural area of our country; above all, it will be a return of love from the children to the Father's love.
>
> With this purpose in mind, a group of friends have formed a committee which is now working energetically for the execution of the project. Numerous friends from Italy and foreign countries have already given not only their enthusiastic support, but also generous donations for carrying out this grandiose work of charity.
>
> We are anxious that all the friends, near and far, should know about the project and be able to contribute according to their means and the intensity of their love which attracts them to San Giovanni Rotondo.
>
> We are sending to everyone this first communication, which should be like the sound of the trumpet to awaken fraternal charity and to have the joy of contributing to this great beneficent work. When it is completed, all together we shall offer it as a homage to the Father of our souls.

Meanwhile, the war had spread to Italy and, to prevent the donations from undergoing a severe devaluation, some holdings were acquired in Lucera. Then, when the war ended and peace returned, the notary public, Girolamo Caggianelli, on October 5, 1946, instituted a social action society at Foggia called *Casa Sollievo della Sofferenza,* which would erect and supervise an institute at San Giovanni Rotondo for the cure and care of the sick and for spiritual assistance.

The civil document was signed by Doctor Sanguinetti, Doctor Kisvarday, Don Giuseppi Orlando, Doctor Eleonora Figna, Doctor Guglielmo Panicali and Pasquale De Meis, all of whom agreed to renounce any and all personal gain.

Later, the following persons became members of the project: Doctor Sanvico, Angela Serritelli, John Telfner, Mario Cacciaglia, Giambattista Sacchetti, Bernardo Patrizi, Daniele Ungaro, Giovanni Pennelli and others. The location selected was the tract of land that had been given by civil authorities to Maria Basilio for the construction of a charitable institution.

After the completion of the legal work and the availability of a suitable terrain, Padre Pio was anxious for the work to start. On May 16 he blessed the cornerstone and on May 19 the first shovel of dirt was turned. The overall supervision was given to the diocesan priest, Don Peppino Orlando. This is the way he recorded the early steps:

> Padre Pio always sat next to me. Every evening he would be nudging me in the side with his elbow, so much so that I tried to avoid sitting near him.
>
> "Have you heard that you are to begin the work?"
>
> "But why must I make people laugh at us behind our backs? Start work on a large hospital without a plan, without a blueprint, without a contractor?"
>
> "You must start the work!"
>
> One evening, just to make him happy, I said to him: "Tomorrow I shall make a road in that rocky terrain donated by Maria Basilio; but listen well: I can make only one road."

Yes; exactly one road. I bought two balls of cord and with twenty men I began the work on a road four meters wide, marking off each side with the taut cord and making two curbs with stones dug out of the rocky soil.

Padre Pio watched us every day from a window in the friary and in the evening I had to brush my cassock because of the dust that came from the day's work. But how happy he was!

Don Peppino was right. They could not begin the work without a plan, without a blueprint, without a contractor. Consequently, sketches were requested, and of those submitted, the one by the civil engineer Candeloro was admired by everyone. However, it was the architect Angelo Lupi who was chosen to make the sketch a reality. Actually, Lupi was some hours short of obtaining his degree, but he was acclaimed as an architectural genius. He recruited and organized workmen who began immediately to level the mountainside. He constructed a lime kiln to extract from stones the lime for the plaster. The tile for the flooring was also made from material that he got from the mountain. Padre Pio's American secretary at the time, Father Dominic Meyer, said of Angelo Lupi that he was "architect, contractor, superintendent and a lot of other things for the new hospital. Through his genius, all manner of necessary equipment and supplies are being made here. This saves a lot of money and gives work to the poor people here." As a matter of fact, Angelo Lupi was so competent and energetic that he was accused to the authorities at Foggia of "the abusive exercise of the profession of an architect."

However, Padre Pio reassured him by saying: "Don't worry, my son. The person who denounced you has received his degree from men. But you have received yours from God." And because of the prestige of Padre Pio, the matter was dropped.

The early donations had made it possible to start construction. The balance sheet for 1948, which was made public, showed that the money had been well spent and the project had provided employment for many people in the region. All sorts of means were used to collect funds for the completion of the project: theatrical presentations, lotteries, raffles, bazaars, etc. In practically every shop and store there was a small box for donations. But to move forward at a faster pace, the intervention of divine providence was needed, and it was granted in response to the supplications of Padre Pio.

In autumn of 1947, a young British economist and journalist, Barbara Ward, came to Rome to write a report on the postwar reconstruction of Italy for her magazine, *The Economist*. While in Italy she was the guest of Marchese Bernardo Patrizi, whom she had known in London. Since he was a great supporter of Padre Pio, and Barbara Ward had expressed a desire to meet the Capuchin stigmatist, the Patrizis offered to accompany her to San Giovanni Rotondo. Possibly the Marchese also thought that Barbara Ward might be in a position to help the work in progress.

When they arrived at San Giovanni Rotondo, Barbara Ward first visited the work site of the hospital, asking many questions and especially how it was being financed and what was the overall cost. Later she met Padre Pio and had a chance to assist at his Mass and have a visit with him. She was greatly impressed by his humility and kindness and she summoned the courage to say: "Father, I have come to ask a grace."

"My daughter," said Padre Pio, "it is God who gives graces."

Barbara Ward continued: "I am a Catholic, but my fiancé is Protestant. I would like him to convert to Catholicism."

"If God wills, he will convert!" said Padre Pio.

"Yes, but when?" she asked.

"If God wills, right now," he concluded.

The young lady was somewhat disappointed. The simple and general statements of Padre Pio were not very reassuring. However, when she returned to London, she had her confidence in Padre Pio restored. On the very day and in the very hour that she was visiting with Padre Pio, her fiancé, Commander Robert

Jackson, was converted to the Catholic faith and received the sacrament of baptism!

Barbara talked at length to Commander Jackson about Padre Pio and she described the construction of the charitable hospital that was being built at San Giovanni Rotondo. Commander Jackson was deputy director of UNRRA, an organization set up to distribute funds for the rebuilding of European countries severely damaged during World War II.

Later, Commander Jackson went to San Giovanni Rotondo to thank Padre Pio. It was a very moving experience for the Commander, and after expressing his gratitude, he said: "Padre, I know that you need funds. I will do what I can to help you get them." Later on, with the help of the widow of Fiorello La Guardia, former mayor of New York City and formerly president of UNRRA, the organization gave $325,000 USA for the construction of the *Casa Sollievo della Sofferenza.*

The UNRRA notified the head of the Italian government about the grant, and he in turn informed the head of the provincial government at Foggia. Surprised to learn that a hospital was already in the process of construction at San Giovanni Rotondo, without the permission of competent government authority, the head of medical services was sent to investigate. A thousand difficulties arose, and there was a danger that the entire work would be halted. Padre Pio energetically defended the assignment of funds by UNRRA. In the end, thanks to the abusive practices of bureaucracy, the grant was reduced to $250,000 USA because the government took an exorbitant percentage for itself.

The providential gift from UNRRA stimulated an upsurge of interest and donations to the project. Doctor Sanguinetti, who considered himself an amateur at building and landscaping, planted thousands of seedling trees that changed the landscape of the mountainside. Practically everyone in the region became involved in the project in one way or another. The creative ideas of Angelo Lupi were gradually realized. The donations from the devout admirers of Padre Pio made a gigantic leap forward.

An Italian workman in the United States, Mario Gambino, had set up a fund for the sick poor and he was able periodically to send large donations in U.S. dollars. Collections were being taken up everywhere.

In the autumn of 1950, Barbara Ward returned to San Giovanni Rotondo. She looked at the magnificent structure and was very pleased with the way they had used the money from UNRRA. When she went into the chapel of the hospital, she found a surprise awaiting her. The face of the Blessed Virgin in the stained-glass window to the right of the altar resembled her own! That was done at the suggestion of Angelo Lupi, who considered Barbara Ward, as all do today, as the *madrina* of the hospital.

On July 26, 1954, Padre Pio blessed the outpatient department, at which time he said:

> Our first thanks go to the Lord, who has willed this work. Then to all the benefactors, near and far, to the instruments of divine providence... Remember that this is the work of charity, and therefore it is necessary to serve here in the spirit of God. I have done nothing; all of you have done it all... I have blessed and encouraged, but you are the workers!

The people smiled at such humility. Padre Pio was deeply moved and very happy. But his happiness was dampened a month later by the death of Doctor Sanguinetti. He mourned deeply. He would have preferred that the Lord did not take from his side that good and faithful friend, that indefatigable worker.

By that time the *Casa* was just about completed. And it was beautiful. To one or another it seemed too luxurious, too richly adorned with expensive marble. To this, Padre Pio would say: "Too luxurious? If I could have done so, I would have made it all of gold... because the sick are Jesus, and what is done for the Lord is always too little."

It was decided to give a juridical basis to the hospital, which had been entrusted to the care of a confraternity of Third

Order Franciscans under the supervision of Padre Pio. The idea was to form a group for professional and spiritual care from among the nursing personnel. Among the religious who had offered their services were the Missionary Sisters of the Sacred Heart. Everything was set for the official inauguration on May 5, 1956, the feast of Pope St. Pius V.

Among the personages present for the occasion were Cardinal Giacomo Lercaro of Bologna, the President of the Italian Senate Merzagora, the Minister of State Braschi, the Minister General of the Capuchin Order, the widow of Guglielmo Marconi, and the operatic tenor Beniamino Gigli.

Cardinal Lercaro had come down to San Giovanni Rotondo in a military plane provided by the Italian Air Force, and after the Mass celebrated by Padre Pio, he said:

> It is useless to say a word when things speak for themselves in such an eloquent manner, but if a comment, or any comment, could be made, I would say to you that on my way here this morning, I thought of the beautiful antiphon: "*Ubi caritas et amor, ibi Deus*" (Where there is charity and love, there is God)… This beautiful statement can also be turned around: "Where God is, there is charity and love." You have all come to San Giovanni Rotondo… God is here, and evidently here also is charity and love.

Shortly thereafter, Padre Pio spoke:

> The *Casa Sollievo della Sofferenza* is completed. I thank the benefactors from every part of the world who have helped. This is what Providence, with your help, has created. I present it to you. Admire it, and together with me, bless the Lord our God!
> Deposited in the earth is a seed which he will warm with the rays of his love. A new militia of renunciation and love has been formed for the glory of God and the consolation of the souls and bodies of the sick. Don't

deprive us of your help; collaborate in this apostolate for the relief of human suffering, and the divine charity, that knows no limits and is the very light of God and of life eternal, will accumulate for each one of you a treasury of graces of which Jesus has made us the heirs on the Cross. This work which you see today is at the beginning of its life, but in order to grow and to reach maturity, it must be nourished, and for that reason it is recommended again to your generosity so that it will not perish from want but will be a hospital city that can cope with the most demanding medical needs and at the same time the ascetical requirements of militant Franciscanism. This is a place of prayer and of science, where human beings should meet one another in Christ Crucified as one flock under one Shepherd.

A stage of the journey has been completed. But we do not stop. We respond conscientiously to the call of God for a good cause, each one doing his duty: I, in the unceasing prayer of a useless servant of our Lord Jesus Christ, and you with the ardent desire to press to your heart all of suffering humanity, to offer it with me to the mercy of the heavenly Father; you with actions illumined by grace, with generosity, perseverance in good, and right intention.

Go forth in humility of spirit and with generous heart. God bless all those who have worked and are working for this *Casa*. May he reward thousands of times over, you and your families in this life and with eternal happiness in the life to come.

We ask the Blessed Virgin of Graces and our Seraphic Father St. Francis to intercede for us in heaven and the Vicar of Christ, the Sovereign Pontiff, to intercede for us on earth so that our prayers will be heard.

There were also interventions by Marchese Sacchetti, the civil engineer Ghisleri, the mayor of San Giovanni Rotondo, Professor Nylin and Doctor Gigliozzi. Then Padre Pio and Cardinal Lercaro together cut the traditional silk ribbon.

At the inauguration of the *Casa Sollievo della Sofferenza*, one of the most prestigious events was an international symposium of the European Society of Cardiology under the chairmanship of Doctor Pietro Valdoni. At the time the president of the Society was Doctor Gustav Nylin of Sweden, who praised the hospital as a magnificent work of charity. During one of the intermissions, the group went over to the friary and surrounded Padre Pio with admiration and affection. At their insistence, he addressed them briefly:

What should I say to you? All of you came into the world as I did, with a mission to fulfill. Notice: I am talking to you about duties at a time in which everyone is talking about rights.

As a religious and a priest, I have a mission to fulfill. As a religious, as a Capuchin, the perfect and loving observance of my rule and of my vows; as a priest, my mission is one of propitiation, to conciliate between God and the human race.

All this can be accomplished if I am in God's grace, but if I am estranged from God, if instead of being a conciliator I fall into the state of one needing propitiation, how can I possibly be a mediator before the All-high?

You have the mission to cure the sick; but if you do not bring love to the bedside, I do not think that medicine will do much good. I have proven this. When I was sick in 1916-1917, in treating me my doctor would first of all say a word of comfort. Love cannot do without words. How can you express your love except with words that bring comfort to the sick?

Later on, I went to a specialist who, without any pleasant words, simply told me that I was consumptive and that I would have more or less one more year to live. I returned home with death in my heart, resigned to the will of God. But as you see, I am still here. The prediction of the specialist was not verified. But not all the sick are like Padre Pio was in 1916-1917.

Bring God to the sick; that is of more value than any other treatment. And the Lord will bless you, all of you, your families and in a special way your work and your patients.

The first patient entered Padre Pio's hospital on May 10 and was assigned to one of the 300 beds. In a short time the hospital was fully functioning. In addition to the outpatient department, there was general surgery and urology, with two operating rooms; medicine and cardiology; orthopedics and trauma; pediatrics; obstetrics and gynecology, with operating room and delivery room; x-ray and laboratory. One year after the opening of the hospital, Padre Pio gave this inspiring talk about his work:

> Blessed be the Lord! The work which you saw last year at the beginning of its life, today completes its first year of life. The *Casa Sollievo della Sofferenza* has opened its arms to several thousand sick bodies and souls so that all the patients without exception can benefit from your charity, from the most prosperous to the most needy…
>
> God has warmed with the rays of his love the seed that was planted. From its birth until today… the work has had to ask for contributions from generous persons, to whom I now express my thanks. Today, with the approval of the Holy Father, the work has gained its autonomy. With providential generosity and solicitude, the Sovereign Pontiff has decreed that the work should have a juridical basis corresponding to the purposes for which it was founded. The Holy Father has granted that there should be a new arrangement as regards its patrimony and that all of its goods should be entrusted to the Franciscan Third Order of *Santa Maria delle Grazie*…
>
> Today we enter the second stage of its journey to maturity… The work again calls upon your generosity so that it can become a hospital city that can meet the most demanding clinical needs. The *Casa* must increase the number of beds. To do this, it will be necessary to

make two new sections, one for women and one for men, where weary and overworked souls and bodies can come to the Lord and find rest. Then, an international center of studies that should enable the medical corps to perfect their professional expertise and their Christian formation. We should complete this work so that it will become a temple of prayer and of science where human beings can meet one another in Christ Crucified as one fold under the one Shepherd.

The members of the work, who in all parts of the world gather together to pray in common, in accordance with the spirit of our Seraphic Father St. Francis and the intentions of the Holy Father, should find here a common house for their prayer groups: priests will find here a cenacle for themselves; men, women and religious will find here houses in which to foster even more their spiritual formation and their ascent to God, so that in faith, detachment and dedication they may live the love of God which is the ultimate consummation of Christian perfection.

Jesus joins to the activity of the Divine Master the activity of a Healer. He is the author of life who once died but now lives and reigns.

If this work were only for the relief of the body, it would be a model clinic, built with the means provided by your extraordinarily generous charity. But it was founded to be a vital summons to the love of God through the invitation to charity.

Here the suffering ought to live the love of God by accepting their affliction, by their serene meditation on their destiny in God.

Here the love of God should be strengthened in the souls of the sick through their love of Jesus Crucified, which will emanate from those who treat the sickness of the body and sickness of the soul. Here the doctors, priests and the recovered will be reservoirs of the love which, the more abundant it is in one, the more copiously it can be communicated to others.

The priests and doctors, dedicated to the exercise of charity towards sick bodies, will feel the burning desire to remain in God's love, so that they and their assistants may all have one common indwelling in him who is Light and Love…

May *Maria Santissima delle Grazie,* who is the Queen to whom every day and many times in the day we manifest our love and of whom we ask her maternal assistance, reign always in the city that will rise here and may she assist all of you. May the Madonna intensify the love of her children for the Vicar of Christ on earth, and one day may she show us Jesus in the splendor of his glory.

The program outlined by Padre Pio became a reality in time. Then, as a faithful son of the Church and as a religious under the vow of poverty, he drew up his last will and testament with the intention of entrusting everything to the Church:

I hereby name the Holy See, and through the Holy See the Sovereign Pontiff at the time, as the heir to all the goods, movable and immovable, in my possession, in whatever way they belong to me and in whatever way they came to me, and also the goods that will accrue from any title or description different from my own, such as: *Opera di Padre Pio da Pietrelcina, Casa Sollievo della Sofferenza, San Giovanni Rotondo.* With the present I revoke any other previous testamentary disposition. *P. Pio of Pietrelcina (Francesco Forgione).*

The *Opera di Padre Pio* came to the attention of the whole world. Further developments followed; for example, the number of departments and the number of beds increased; the medical equipment became ever more sophisticated and up to date. In a short time the former statistics and the balance sheet were out of date, due to the continuous growth and development.

That "seed" planted in the earth by the wounded hands of the stigmatized Capuchin, warmed by the rays of the love of God, and nourished by such generous charity, grew from day to day, expanded and improved. It can no longer be called simply a hospital but, as its founder desired, it is truly a "hospital city," technically capable of responding to the most urgent clinical needs. In addition, it has become a center of medical research.

25

PRAYER GROUPS

$\mathscr{T}$HE *Casa Sollievo della Sofferenza,*
a cathedral of charity, had a beautiful and powerful foundation:
the prayer groups of Padre Pio. By his life and works Padre Pio
had on numerous occasions proclaimed love and obedience to
the Church and to its visible head. And immediately after World
War II, he gave another proof of his sincere sentiments that were
nourished by the interventions by the Vicar of Christ.

During the second worldwide conflict, Pope Pius XII,
realizing how great was the need for prayer, had launched an
appeal to all the faithful:

> Pray, pray, pray! Prayer is the key to the treasury of
> God; it is the weapon of combat and of victory in every
> struggle for good and against evil. What can prayer not
> do, adoring, making propitiation, petitioning, giving
> thanks.
>
> We need strong, compact legions of people who,
> keeping themselves closely united to Christ, receive the
> Bread of life at least once a month and encourage others
> to follow their example.

With these words, pronounced on February 17, 1942, the
Pope urged the assembly and formation of prayer groups among
the faithful who, "freed from the slavery of human respect, will

conform their lives and their activity to the commandments of God and the precepts of Christ."

From his boyhood days, when Padre Pio recited the rosary with the family in front of the fireplace, he had dreamed of forming prayer groups. That dream was revived during the first years of his residence at San Giovanni Rotondo when, during the long evenings in winter, the friars were seated around the community fire in the friary of *Santa Maria delle Grazie*.

The words and the promise of Christ frequently came back to his mind: "If two of you join your voices on earth to pray for anything whatever, it shall be granted you by my Father in heaven. Where two or three are gathered in my name, there am I in their midst" (Mt 18:19-20).

Promptly and enthusiastically he responded to the exhortation of Pope Pius XII. He assembled his spiritual sons and daughters, who were already accustomed to prayer, and he said to them: "Let's give ourselves something to do and let's roll up our sleeves. Let's be among the first to answer this appeal of the Holy Father."

That is the way Padre Pio's prayer groups began, and under the mysterious power of grace, they soon spread throughout Italy. They did not have definite structure or precise rules. In the name of Padre Pio, they assembled periodically, once or twice a month, under the guidance of a priest. Usually they recited the rosary in common, assisted at Mass and received Holy Communion.

Through his faithful collaborators, Padre Pio's words of encouragement reached everyone. "Don't grow weary of praying. That is the essential thing! Prayer can do violence to the heart of God and obtains graces… It is the best weapon that we have… It is the key that opens the heart of God."

On a geographical map a luminous star was pasted at each place where there was a prayer group. Soon the map shone with hundreds of lights, hundreds of stars. Thanks to the teaching of Padre Pio, the prayer movement flourished wherever the Christian life was fervent. It stimulated the weak and it reached out to those who were away from the Church. Eventually it spread to foreign countries; first to Switzerland, then to France, the United States, Germany, Belgium, Luxembourg.

Padre Pio liked to meet his prayer groups in the *Casa Sollievo della Sofferenza*, and on March 5, 1966, he told them in a discourse:

> The prayer groups, now scattered throughout the world and affiliated to the *Casa Sollievo della Sofferenza*, are the advance guard of this city of charity... Christ himself is present every time the groups gather together for prayer and the eucharistic *Agape*, under the guidance of their pastors and spiritual directors.
>
> It is prayer that unites all good souls, that renews the conscience, sustains the *Casa Sollievo della Sofferenza*, comforts the suffering, heals the sick, sanctifies the work, inspires the medical assistants, gives moral strength and Christian resignation in human suffering... Pray much, my children, pray always, without ever tiring, because it is to prayer that I entrust this work, which God has willed and which will remain and prosper, thanks to the help of Divine Providence and the spiritual and charitable contributions of all souls who pray.

Following the example of Padre Pio, the prayer groups inserted themselves as the ferment of the interior life in the structure of the local church or diocese. The Padre never tired of repeating his recommendations. "May they be united; may they never tire of doing good; may they be obedient and respectful to all the members of the hierarchy, constant and persevering. Do not do anything without the approval and permission of the bishops and priests. Do everything in common agreement, and obey, obey!"

Cardinal Giacomo Lercaro of Bologna, in a discourse given on April 25, 1960, stated that a prayer group is "a force, an immense force, a force that assists the omnipotence of God and his goodness, a force that knows that it is not deceived."

Padre Pio wanted his prayer groups to be faithful also to liturgical and community prayer. All the members should be concerned about their own sanctification and the sanctification of others, giving witness to Christ, evangelizing, under the guidance of the Magisterium of the Church.

The first public recognition by an eminent personage of what was pouring out of the heart of Padre Pio, came from the Vicar of Christ, Pope Paul VI, who addressed the International Congress of Prayer Groups in Rome on September 24, 1975:

> Among the many good and great things that he has accomplished, Padre Pio has founded this great company, this river of persons who pray and who, following his example and in the hope of his spiritual help, dedicate themselves to the Christian life and give witness of communion in prayer, in charity, in poverty of spirit and in the dynamism of the Christian profession.

The same Pope, on June 25, 1978, singled out the prayer groups of Padre Pio as "little cells of ecclesial life… that diffuse in our world, permeated with materialistic personalism, the vivifying oxygen of the spiritual heights."

We add to the foregoing significant passage the words of Pope John Paul II to the 2000 prayer groups of Padre Pio assembled in Rome on October 1, 1983:

> Your presence and your Christian commitment are indissolubly bound to the personality and work of Padre Pio of Pietrelcina, the humble Capuchin friar who, for fifty years, in the convent of San Giovanni Rotondo, lived and carried out his religious consecration to God almost exclusively in constant daily fervent prayer and in the ministry of the sacrament of reconciliation, guiding and directing thousands of the faithful.
>
> Padre Pio left this life in September of 1968; but the mysterious fruitfulness of his long life as a priest and religious, son of St. Francis of Assisi, still continues to

act, we may say, with visible crescendo, and in particular in two works that are typically "his" because they
were born of his great heart, open to love of God and
the brethren: the prayer groups and the *Casa Sollievo
della Sofferenza.*

On May 3, 1986, the Secretary of State, Cardinal Agostino
Casaroli, approved the statutes of the prayer groups of Padre
Pio. He approved and reconfirmed the basic principles of Franciscan spirituality laid down by Padre Pio when he founded the
prayer groups. The letter then enumerates five principles which
should be developed in the Padre Pio prayer groups:

1. Full and unconditional adherence to the teaching of the
   Catholic Church, under the guidance of the Pope and the
   bishops.
2. Obedience to the Pope and the bishops, for whom the
   spokesman within the prayer group is the spiritual director (priest) named by the bishop.
3. Prayer with the Church, for the Church and in the Church,
   with active participation in the liturgical and sacramental
   life, which is the summit of intimate communion with
   God.
4. Reparation by sharing in the sufferings of Christ, according to the teaching of St. Paul.
5. Actual and operative charity for the relief of the suffering
   and the needy as an exercise of the love of God.

The fortieth anniversary of the beginning of the prayer
groups was celebrated on September 29, 1990, with an audience
with Pope John Paul II, who said:

> Before you is a unique, outstanding model of the
> priest, Padre Pio of Pietrelcina, who helped so many
> souls find the school which teaches truth and love.
> What was the source of the light which he succeeded
> in communicating to those he met? Certainly prayer,

listening to God, long penances and, above all, the celebration of Holy Mass, which constituted the heart of his life.

Sometimes people are tempted to say that prayer is not necessary; they are led to think that life's problems can be solved only through concrete action.

While a daily involvement in the various fields of human endeavor is indispensable, yet the teachings of the Gospel and the example of the saints — especially the witness of Padre Pio — remind us that even in solitude, silence and the hidden life one can effectively help one's neighbor.

Only in heaven will we be able to know, for example, how much the *Casa Sollievo della Sofferenza* in San Giovanni Rotondo is indebted to the insistent prayers of Padre Pio and other countless faithful; these prayers have remained hidden from people's eyes, but not from God's.

Therefore, may all of you, wherever you are, be silent adorers of the Divine Mystery and apostles of his mercy. Follow the example of Padre Pio; imitate his constant search for intimacy with the Lord, since this is the sole secret of spiritual life. Like him, walk down the road of authentic conversion, of voluntary penance and trusting abandonment to Providence.

Look to Mary who, while she contemplated in her heart the extraordinary events which she was called to live (Lk 2:51), was attentive to and concerned for the concrete needs of her neighbor (Jn 2:1ff).

I sincerely hope that each of you will remain faithful to the teachings of your Father, who still today, I am sure, continues to lovingly watch over his spiritual sons and daughters.

On the tenth anniversary of the canonical approval of the prayer groups, celebrated in St. Peter's Square in Rome, Pope John Paul II renewed his exhortation to the members:

In Padre Pio you rightly admire a dedicated *servant of the Church*... I again invite each one of you to imitate the ecclesial spirit of the beloved Padre Pio, deepening your relationship with your pastors, participating actively in the initiatives of the parochial and diocesan communities, and offering your highly esteemed contribution of prayer, charity and Gospel witness to the life of the diocese to which you belong.

The members of the Padre Pio prayer groups, spread throughout the world, now number more than 500,000. Blessed by the Pope and the bishops and inserted into the cellular organism of the Church, they are nourished in faith, hope and charity by the marvelous example of their founder, diffusing in every area a message of intense spirituality and salvation.

26

FROM PRAYER TO ACTION

$\mathcal{A}$LTHOUGH HE WAS DEEPLY IMMERSED in God, Padre Pio was no stranger to the human problems that surrounded him. Through his ministry in the confessional, he constantly encountered the material and spiritual needs of so many brothers and sisters. He came into contact with the same problems and needs in his apostolate in the *Casa Sollievo della Sofferenza* and with the prayer groups. But that was not enough for him; he wanted to do much more. He began to move his spiritual sons and daughters to action. He had already formed them in the practice of prayer and he had wanted to enroll them in the membership of the Franciscan Third Order so that their souls would be inflamed with the enthusiasm and warmth of the *Poverello* of Assisi. Now he wanted them to give witness in the social ambience. The love of God must diffuse itself; it must act, "with an eye on the earth."

What was needed in San Giovanni Rotondo was institutions for the education of children and the formation of young people. Padre Pio constantly urged the superior, Padre Carmelo, to do something about the problem. At first a space was rented and the Franciscan Third Order inaugurated a formation center; and then the Franciscan Sisters of Ozzano Emilia took charge of a training school for girls. On December 17, 1957, the cornerstone was blessed for a new building which would house a professional training school for girls under the direction of the Franciscan Sisters. There the students would receive training in cooking and sewing.

During those years various sects were very active in proselytizing the Italian people. One of these groups wanted to build a meeting hall near the friary in San Giovanni Rotondo, but they ran into obstacles. They finally settled in the district of Sant'Onofrio, and in a short time they had constructed a place for their gatherings and for organizing their campaign for the "re-education" of the people. They also opened a kindergarten.

Padre Pio suffered very much as a result of those developments. He knew, for example, that the children were exposed to virulent criticism of the faith and rejection of the Madonna. Red with indignation, he went to the superior and said: "Do something quickly! Go in my name to the archbishop and get permission to open a kindergarten right near theirs. Don't be afraid! The Madonna will be with you."

Padre Carmelo went to Archbishop Andrea Cesarano and he got the permission, but he was still perplexed and confused. Once more Padre Pio went on the offensive and promised to pray, saying that it was necessary to do and act as Moses did. The school was opened in a rented locale and was later transferred to the residence of the Capuchin Sisters, who had come from Sicily. As a result, the offending group had to close their kindergarten and move to another area. Then, through the efforts of Padre Pio, a third school, *Pace e Bene*, was opened in that same place; not only a kindergarten but a professional training school for girls. Thus, Padre Pio carried on the attack not only with prayers but with action. His example prompted some of his spiritual children to say: "Now is the hour to leave the warmth of the sacristy and fight like lions!"

Padre Pio's activity in the social sphere was supernaturally motivated and evangelically justified. One day he noticed a long line of young people at the friary. When he asked who they were, he was told that they were unemployed young people who had come to the friary asking help. Padre Pio was surprised and indignant. "What! Young people twenty years old begging for alms? And when are they going to work?"

Then, going to the superior, he said: "It would be better if you would teach them an art or a trade. Do something! Go to our friends in Rome. It is absolutely necessary to act."

Padre Carmelo encountered any number of obstacles and difficulties, but with the help of Padre Pio he was able to overcome them one by one. On January 26, 1958, thanks to a concession by the military, a professional training school was opened on the site of the Amendola airfield. Later the school was moved into new and more ample quarters so that it was able to provide employment for hundreds of young men from the region.

Padre Pio also inspired a number of other enterprises, and among them, a cooperative for foodstuffs, a cenacle for Franciscan culture, a center for auto repair, a monastery for Capuchin nuns, a monumental *Via Crucis*, a home for old people. All of these activities were the result of his exceptional apostolate and his ardent charity.

27

EXPRESSIONS OF HIS SPIRITUALITY

*P*ADRE PIO DEMONSTRATED IN A DRAMA-tic and profound manner our need of the supernatural, our innate need for transcendence and the infinite. And this is evident in the vast expanses of his spirit, his soul, his heart. He possessed a very delicate and ample sensitivity that led him to live the spiritual life with a personal modality, an individual distinctiveness, and a specificity all his own. It was "his" spirituality, but with the common denominator (common to every man, to every believer) of a substantial unity of spiritual and supernatural elements in an "ecclesial" context.

All of it was "*ad modum recipientis recipitur*" and (if one may say so) "*et exprimitur.*" (Everything is received — and expressed — in accordance with the personality of the one who receives it.)

Padre Pio loved the Church as the depositary of the mystery of salvation. "I want to live and die in the Church," he once said. And he suffered very much when he got wind of the numerous disputes in Church circles. He contested the challengers. He did not want any deviation from traditional Catholic doctrine. Hence, his spirituality was expressed with an ardent love of the Eucharist, a filial love of the Madonna, an unconditional love for the Church and its visible head, a tender devotion to the guardian angel, the saints and the souls in purgatory. In 1929, in obedience to Padre Agostino, he had started to write his *Diario*, and it opened with these words:

> In the name of our Lord Jesus Christ. Personal daily devotions. Not less than four hours of meditation, and these ordinarily on the life of our Lord: birth, passion and death. Novenas to the Madonna of Pompeii, to St. Joseph, to St. Michael the Archangel, to St. Anthony, to our Father St. Francis, to the Sacred Heart of Jesus, to St. Rita, to St. Teresa of Jesus. Daily no less than five entire rosaries [fifteen decades] (*Epistolario*, IV, 986).

His meditations were usually made before the tabernacle. Padre Pio was strongly and mysteriously drawn to Jesus in the Eucharist. In his letters he has written passages that give some indication of the depth of his love:

> My heart feels drawn by a higher power before being united with him in the Blessed Sacrament. I have such hunger and thirst before receiving him that it would take little more for me to die of longing... And rather than remain satisfied after I have received the Sacrament, this hunger and thirst increases even more. At the moment that I am in possession of this greatest good, then yes, the plenitude of sweetness is truly so great that I almost say to Jesus: Enough! I cannot stand any more! I forget that I am even in this world. The mind and heart desire nothing more...
>
> I sometimes ask myself if there are souls that do not feel their chest burn with divine fire, especially at the moment that they find themselves before him in the Blessed Sacrament. It seems to me to be impossible, particularly if the individual is a priest or religious. Perhaps the souls who say that they do not experience this divine fire, are not aware of it because their hearts are so much larger. It is only with this benign interpretation that I can relate to them, in order not to impute to them the shameful label of being liars (*Epistolario*, II, 317).

One day, while praying in the choir of the church, Padre Pio heard Jesus lament as follows:

> With what ingratitude my love is repaid by ungrateful men! I would be less offended by them if I had loved them less. My Father does not want to put up with them anymore. I would stop loving them, but... (and here Jesus is silent and sighs, and then begins again) but alas! My heart was made to love. Weak and sinful men make no effort to overcome temptations; rather, they delight in their iniquity. Souls greatly loved by me, when put to the test, come to me less frequently. The weak ones abandon me in despair and the strong ones gradually fall away.
>
> I remain all alone in the church, night and day. They no longer care about the Sacrament of the altar; they never talk about this Sacrament of love; and those who do speak, alas, do so with coldness and indifference.
>
> My heart is forgotten; no one cares about my love; I am always sad. My house has become for many a theater for entertainment. Even my ministers, whom I have always regarded with special affection and have loved as the pupil of my eye, they should comfort my heart so full of grief; they should help me in the redemption of souls; but instead (who would believe it!) I receive ingratitude and neglect. I see many of them who... (here he became silent, because his sobs choked off his voice) with hypocritical actions betray me with sacrilegious Communions (*Epistolario*, I, 342).

Padre Pio adored the mystery of the Eucharist and was stunned at the humility of the God-Man. He once wrote to Raffaelina Cerase:

> He who is one thing with the Father, he who is the love and delight of the eternal Creator, although he knew that all that he would do on earth would be well-received and ratified by his Father in heaven, even asked

permission to remain with us!

What an excess of love for us in the Son and at the same time what an excess of humility in asking us to permit him to remain with us until the end of the world! But also what an excess of love for us in the Father, after having seen the miserable treatment, permits his beloved Son to remain with us and every day to be the object of new insults!

How could such a good Father have consented to this? Did it not suffice, O eternal Father, to have your permission once for your beloved Son to be given as a victim to those Jews who were so hostile to him? How could you ever have consented that he should still remain with us, to see him every day in the unworthy hands of so many bad priests, worse even than those Jews who were so hostile to him?

Father, how can your compassionate heart bear to see your only-begotten Son neglected and even disdained by so many unworthy Christians?... O God, who will come to the defense of this meek Lamb, who never opened his mouth for his own sake but only for us? Father, I cannot ask you to take Jesus from our midst. How would I live without this eucharistic food? Father, I entreat you, either quickly put an end to the world or put an end to the sins that are continually committed against the adorable Person of your only-begotten Son (*Epistolario,* II, 343).

Also, while he was hearing confessions, Padre Pio constantly turned his gaze to the tabernacle. In the evening he devoutly recited the "Visit to Jesus in the Blessed Sacrament" composed by St. Alphonsus Liguori. He wanted everyone to be experiencing the same love and to that end he would exhort them as follows:

> In the course of the day, when you can't do anything more, just call upon Jesus. Do this even in the midst of your activities... and he will come and remain united to

your soul through his grace and his holy love. Fly to the tabernacle in spirit when you cannot do so physically, and there pour forth your ardent longings, and speak and pray and embrace the beloved of souls. (*Epistolario*, III, 448).

Padre Pio considered the Holy Eucharist as "the great means for aspiring to perfection." He wanted his spiritual sons and daughters to approach the altar daily with faith and love to receive "the bread of angels." Once one of them asked him: "Father, when you are no longer with us, what shall we do without you?"

He responded: "Go before the tabernacle; in Jesus you will also find me!"

The love of Jesus in the Blessed Sacrament was, for Padre Pio, intimately connected with a trusting, filial and unbounded love for the Madonna. He once wrote to Padre Agostino:

> This most tender Mother, in her great mercy, wisdom and goodness, has willed to "chastise" me in an exalted manner by pouring into my heart so many graces that when I find myself in her presence and that of Jesus, I am forced to cry out: "Where am I? Who is here with me?" I feel as if I am burning up, without any flames. I feel that I am closely bound to the Son through the Mother, without seeing the chains that hold me fast... I feel that I am constantly dying and yet forever alive (*Epistolario*, I, 357).

He desired that other souls should also enjoy this indissoluble bond. One of the aspirations that he frequently repeated was: "May this dearest Mother unite us so closely to Jesus that we cannot let ourselves be enticed and ensnared by anything in this world" (*Epistolario*, I, 606).

Love for the Mother of Jesus flourished in him since the days of his early childhood within the confines of the family. In the parish church of Pietrelcina, he found the statue of the *Madonna della Libera* to be beautiful in her flowing garments, regal in stature, with a tender maternal gaze and a delicate smile. He would remain immobile before her, engaged in a mutual dialogue. To the Virgin of virgins he had offered his chastity and his entire being. When he would return from the farm, he would bring a bouquet of the most beautiful and perfumed flowers of the field for her who had captured his heart.

With the passing of the years, his love for the heavenly Mother, whom he loved to call *Mammina,* grew more and more fervent. He especially loved her title as the Immaculate, but everything about the Madonna — her beauty, her perfection, her goodness, her example — drew him to her. On one occasion when he was in ecstatic prayer, he murmured: "*Mammina mia!* How beautiful you are! How splendid! I love you so much... so much!"

Every year the month of May, the month of Mary, brought him great joy. He would go to great pains to honor the Madonna and to get others to honor the woman who gave her consent to the incarnation of the Word. In May, 1912, he wrote to Padre Agostino:

> This month preach well on the sweetness and beauty of Mary... How many times I have entrusted to this Mother the painful anxieties of my anxious heart. And how many times she has consoled me!... Poor *Mammina,* how much she loves me! I have experienced it anew at the beginning of this beautiful month. With what great attention she accompanied me to the altar this morning. It seemed to me that she had nothing else to think about but me, filling my heart with holy sentiments. I felt a mysterious fire in my heart, which I could not understand. I felt the need to apply ice in order to extinguish the fire that was consuming me.
>
> I would like to have a voice so strong that I could call all the sinners of the world to love the Madonna. But since that is not in my power, I have prayer and I shall continue to pray to my guardian angel to fulfill that office (*Epistolario,* I, 276s).

At San Giovanni Rotondo he spent many hours in prayer before the image of *Santa Maria delle Grazie*. He asked her heavenly intervention on behalf of those who had come to him. And when he was presented with an especially difficult case, he would say: "Here we need the Madonna." She was the one who directed his thoughts, suggested how he should act, and inflamed his heart. He went to her under a variety of titles: Mediatrix, Auxiliatrix, Advocate. He loved to contemplate her at the foot of the Cross, and he would say of her:

> The sorrowful Virgin obtains for us from her most holy Son the ability to penetrate ever more deeply into the mystery of the Cross and to be inebriated with the sufferings of Jesus. The greatest proof of love consists in suffering for the beloved, and since the Son of God endured so many sufferings out of pure love, there is no doubt that any cross carried for him becomes lovable to the degree of one's love. May the most holy Virgin obtain for us a love of the Cross, of suffering, of sorrows, and may she who was the first to practice the Gospel in all its perfection, in all its severity, even before it was written, obtain for us on this very day the stimulus to come close to her.
>
> Let us endeavor, like so many elect souls, to follow this blessed Mother, to walk always close to her, not following any other path that leads to life except the one trod by our Mother (*Epistolario*, I, 602).

He once wrote to a spiritual daughter who had asked him to say something about the Madonna: "You should realize that Jesus, who is the source of living water, cannot come to us without a channel, and the channel is Mary. Jesus comes to us only through the Blessed Virgin. Let us imitate the Virgin in holy humility and in prudence. May the Madonna make you experience all her love. Let us abandon ourselves to the hands of the heavenly Mother if we want to find peace and well-being."

Padre Pio expressed his Marian devotion by his constant and practically uninterrupted recitation of the rosary. He always had the rosary in his hands. He considered it a powerful weapon for putting the devil to flight, for overcoming temptation, for conquering the heart of God, and for obtaining graces through the Madonna. "This prayer," he said, "is a summary of our faith; the basis of our hope; the outpouring of our charity."

With the rosary, Padre Pio meditated and contemplated the Gospel foundations of the mystery of salvation. He had mentioned several times that some persons had stated that the rosary was out of fashion, that it had been surpassed by other forms of prayer, but this only made him speak more forcefully in defense of the rosary:

> Let us do what we have always done, what our fathers have done, and all will be well. Satan always tries to destroy this prayer, but he will never succeed. It is the prayer of those who are victorious. It is the prayer that the Madonna taught us, as Jesus taught us the *Pater noster*…

Padre Pio was once asked how the rosary should be recited and he answered: "Pay attention to the *Ave Maria*, the salutation made to the Virgin in the mystery that is being contemplated. She was present in all the mysteries of the Rosary; she participated in all of them with love and sorrow."

The Madonna showed that she was pleased with the love and devotion that Padre Pio had for her. When the "pilgrim statue" of Our Lady of Fatima arrived in Italy, to be taken to various cities throughout the land, Padre Pio was overjoyed and he set to work at once to prepare the people for the statue's arrival in the region. Every day he addressed the crowds through a microphone in his cell, giving them a spiritual meditation and exhortation. For some months he had been bedridden because of pleurisy and several times he had to suffer the painful treatment of draining the pleural effusion.

Finally, on August 5, 1959, the statue arrived at San Giovanni Rotondo and was placed in the church. The next day he was taken in a wheelchair to venerate the image. He kissed the statue and placed a newly blessed rosary in the hands of the Madonna. Then he prayed to her with intense fervor, but soon he had to be taken back to his cell because he was on the verge of collapse.

At the end of the visit of the statue, it was taken to the various departments of the *Casa Sollievo della Sofferenza* and then taken to the next stop by helicopter. The pilot circled the church and the friary three times, as Padre Pio watched from the window of his cell. Then, weeping, he addressed the Blessed Virgin: "Madonna, *Mamma mia,* you have come to Italy, and I am sick. Now you are going and you are leaving me still sick." At that precise instant he was seized with an intense trembling, and he immediately felt so well that he wanted to celebrate Mass in the church. That evening Doctor Gasparrini gave him a thorough examination and declared that he was perfectly well. Padre Pio simply said, with extreme candor: "The Madonna healed me!"

Padre Pio had a profound love for the Church, which he saw as the People of God, the Spouse of Christ and his tender Mother. He prayed and encouraged others to pray for the Church and for the visible head of the Church, the Vicar of Christ on earth. Here is a sampling of expressions taken from his letters:

> Let us pray for the holy Church, our most tender Mother.
> Let us pray that the Lord will disperse the dense clouds that are gathering on the horizon of the Church.
> For me, after Jesus, there is only the Pope.

He was constantly offering sacrifices for the Holy Father and he always had a photo of him in his cell, with a light shining on it. "I want my prayer groups," he said, "to pray always, not only for my intentions, but for all the intentions of priests, bishops and the Pope, whom I love as I love Jesus."

When the renowned scientist, Enrico Medi, visited San Giovanni Rotondo, Padre Pio once said to him: "Enrico, when you go back to Rome, the next time you have an audience with the Pope, tell him that I would give my life for him with great joy."

After hearing these words from Professor Medi, Pope Pius XII said: "No, Professor; thank Padre Pio, but at this moment his life is needed more than mine."

The love of Padre Pio for the Church was also evident in the way in which he received cardinals, bishops, representatives of ecclesiastical offices, from whom he always asked a blessing. Secondly, his sentiments were exemplified in his docile, blind and silent obedience to all who commanded him in the name of the Church. When he was severely limited in the exercise of his priestly ministry, he simply said: "I will obey without opening my mouth, because I am a devoted son of holy obedience." On another occasion he said: "Sweet is the hand of the Church even when it strikes, because it is the hand of a Mother."

When he was informed that Emanuele Brunatto was determined to publish a book he had written, which cast a cloud over some men in the Church, Padre Pio wrote to him to dissuade him:

> If you truly love me as a father, don't continue doing what they tell me you are doing for me and on my behalf, because it will do harm to some persons in Holy Mother Church and to the Capuchin Order, of which I am a devoted son. You cannot love the son and still hurt the mother. Entrust everything with faith into the hands of God and leave everything in the loving hands of providence (*Epistolario*, IV, 747s).

After the promulgation of *Humanae Vitae*, Pope Paul VI suffered a great deal because of the negative reaction in Catholic circles. Under those circumstances Padre Pio wanted to express his total adherence and that of his spiritual sons and daughters to the infallible Magisterium of the Church. On September 12,

1968, with fervent sentiments of piety, obedience and filial devotion, he wrote to Paul VI:

> Your Holiness: I avail myself of the meeting of Your Holiness with the capitular Fathers to unite myself spiritually with my confreres and humbly to place at your feet my affectionate homage, all my devotion for your august person, in an act of faith, love and obedience to the dignity of him whom you represent on earth. The Capuchin Order has always been on the front line in love, fidelity, obedience and devotion to the Apostolic See. I pray the Lord that it will remain and continue in its tradition of religious austerity, evangelical poverty, faithful observance of the rule and constitutions, while renewing its vitality and interior spirit in accordance with the directives of the Second Vatican Council, to be ever prompt in serving the needs of Holy Mother Church, at the bidding of Your Holiness.
>
> I know that your heart is suffering much these days for the Church, for peace in the world, for the numerous needs of people, but especially for the lack of obedience in some, especially Catholics, to the lofty teaching which you, with the help of the Holy Spirit and in the name of God, are giving us. I offer you my prayers and daily sufferings, a small but sincere contribution from the least of your sons, that the Lord will comfort you with his grace to continue along the straight and arduous path in the defense of eternal truth, which can never change with the changing times.
>
> Also, in the name of my spiritual sons and daughters and the prayer groups I thank you for the clear and precise statement you have given us, and I reaffirm my faith, my unconditional obedience to your enlightened directives.
>
> May the Lord grant the triumph of truth, peace to his Church, tranquillity to all the people on earth, health and prosperity to Your Holiness, so that, having dissipated

these passing clouds, the kingdom of God may triumph in all hearts, thanks to your apostolic work as supreme Shepherd of all Christianity.

Prostrate at your feet, I ask you to bless me and my confreres, my spiritual sons and daughters, the prayer groups, my sick, and all the initiatives for good that in the name of Jesus and with your protection we are endeavoring to complete.

The most humble son of Your Holiness, P. Pio, Capuchin.

In the audience granted by Paul VI to the Definitors of the General Chapter of the Capuchins on February 20, 1971, he uttered one of the most beautiful and significant statements concerning Padre Pio: "Look at the fame that Padre Pio has had! He has gathered around himself a worldwide clientèle. Why is that? Perhaps because he was a philosopher, because he was a wise man, because he had means at his disposal? Because he celebrated Mass with great humility, heard confessions from dawn to dusk, and bore — it's difficult to say — the wounds of our Lord. He was a man of prayer and suffering."

Padre Pio had an affectionate, delicate and respectful devotion to his guardian angel. His "good angel" was always at hand, showing himself to be obedient, punctual and precise. A great teacher of holiness, his guardian angel invisibly guided his soul in the practice of all the virtues. Thanks to the action and assistance of his invisible friend, Padre Pio was able to be victorious in the terrible struggle against the forces of evil and avoid the snares of the devil. Likewise, through his angel he was given special gifts: to read and understand foreign languages, to read hearts, to send and receive messages. Padre Pio has left a written account describing how he would wait for "my little companion in my infancy to come and wake me and together sing the morning praise to the beloved of our hearts" (*Epistolario*, I, 308).

Padre Pio had such an ardent love for his guardian angel that he tried to transmit it to his spiritual sons and daughters. This is what he wrote to Raffaelina Cerase:

O Raffaelina! What a great consolation to know that one is always under the protection of a heavenly spirit who does not abandon us even when we offend God! How sweet is this great truth for the soul of the believer! Whom can the devout soul fear who is striving to love God, having always with it such a renowned defender? Was he perhaps one of those who, together with St. Michael, up there in paradise, defended the honor of God against Satan and all the other rebellious spirits, and in the end conquered them and cast them into hell?

Well, you know that he is still powerful in fighting against Satan and his cohorts. His charity has not lessened and he can never fail to defend us. Cultivate the beautiful habit of thinking of him always. Near to us there is a heavenly spirit who never leaves us for an instant, from the cradle to the grave. He guides us, he protects us as a friend, a brother; he always consoles us, especially at times when we are sad.

Know, Raffaelina, that this good angel prays for you, offers to God all your good works, all your pure and holy desires. At times when you feel you are all alone and abandoned, do not complain that you do not have a friendly spirit to whom you can open your heart and to whom you can entrust your sorrows. For goodness sake, do not forget this invisible companion who is always at hand to listen to you and always ready to console you.

O wonderful intimacy; O blessed companionship! If all men would only understand and appreciate this marvelous gift that God, in the excess of his love for men, has given to us in this heavenly spirit... Call upon your guardian angel and repeat the beautiful prayer: "Angel of God, assigned as my guardian by the goodness of the heavenly Father, enlighten me and protect me, now and always." How great will be the consolation, Raffaelina, when at the hour of death your soul will see the good angel who has accompanied you throughout your life and took such tender care of you! May this sweet thought make you ever more devoted to the Cross of Jesus, which is what the good angel desires of you. May the eagerness to see this inseparable companion of your whole life arouse in you that charity which will prompt you to desire to leave this earthly body. O what a holy and salutary thought it is to see our good angel! (*Epistolario*, II, 403s).

To those spiritual sons and daughters who were not able to meet with Padre Pio in person, he would say: "If you need me, send your guardian angel to me." He was kept busy, day and night, listening to the messages brought to him by the angels.

Finally, Padre Pio had been taught first by his mother and then by the parish priest at Pietrelcina that the souls in purgatory can be helped by our prayers and good works. He took this upon himself as part of his vocation, to shorten or alleviate the sufferings of the departed souls. He offered himself as a victim for the "Church suffering," which he remembered in every Mass that he celebrated.

He had his own particular way of giving expression to this devotion. On the landing of the internal stairway of the friary at San Giovanni Rotondo there was and there still is a notice bearing the title, "A brief and easy method for offering suffrages for the souls in purgatory." Nearby was a wooden box containing two compartments in which there were numbered disks similar to those used in a lottery or raffle. Every time Padre Pio ascended or descended the stairs, he would stop on the landing and take a disk from the first compartment in the wooden box. Looking at the number on the disk, he would check to see to which category of souls the number pertained. Then, placing the disk in the second compartment of the box, he would proceed on his way, praying for the designated departed souls.

To show how efficacious were the prayers of Padre Pio for the departed souls, it is said that one evening, after supper, when the friary was closed and the doors all locked, voices were heard shouting at the entrance to the cloister: "Viva Padre Pio! Viva Padre Pio!"

The superior at the time called the Brother Porter and told him to get those people out of the friary. The Brother did as he was told, but when he reached the entrance to the friary, it was empty and the front door was bolted. So he reported to the superior that there was no one there.

The following day the superior asked Padre Pio for an explanation. In all simplicity, Padre Pio stated that the voices heard at the entrance to the cloister were the voices of soldiers who had died in the war and were thanking him for the suffrages he offered for them.

Not only did he offer suffrages for the souls in purgatory; he also prayed to the souls of the blessed in heaven. "O holy souls! You who are now free of all anxiety and anguish and are enjoying the happiness of heaven in the torrent of divine delights, how I envy you! Since you are at the fountain of life and you see me dying of thirst in this miserable land, be so kind as to give me some of that fresh water... be so good as to come to my aid" (*Epistolario*, I, 676s).

28

UNDENIABLE FACTS

$\mathcal{I}$N ADDITION TO THE EXTRAORDINARY gifts that the Lord bestowed on Padre Pio in such profusion, his reputation for sanctity was based also on his virtues and the prodigious results that were attributed to his intercession. The press reported every happening in great detail. These were simply the facts, undeniable and inexplicable. Small groups would gather in the square in front of the church to report anything extraordinary. People began to come from all over with all kinds of afflictions, both physical and spiritual, to seek a cure or simply to ask for prayers.

One of the best known cures attributed to the intercession of Padre Pio was "the miracle of Ribera," named after a small town near Palermo, Sicily. The subject of the cure was a little girl named Gemma Di Giorgi, who was born in 1939 with a congenital defect. She had no pupils in her eyes and hence was totally blind. Her mother had taken her to a famous doctor in Palermo but he told her that the child would never be able to see. Eventually the young girl was taken to Padre Pio, who blessed her eyes. Thereafter she gradually began to be able to see, so that by 1971 it was reported that she could read and write like any normal person.

Giuseppe Canaponi, a workman 34 years old, had collided with a truck while driving to work on his motorcycle. He suffered a skull fracture, fractured ribs and a multiple fracture of his left leg. After a long period of recuperation and various therapies he still had not recovered the complete use of his left leg. In fact, the knee was locked and rigid; but three years after the accident he was in the church of the Capuchins in San Giovanni Rotondo and at Padre Pio's confessional he discovered that he was able to bend his knee and kneel in a normal fashion.

A young girl by the name of Italia Di Chiara was wearing braces as a result of polio during her infancy. At the command of Padre Pio, she removed the braces and immediately began to walk and move around, completely cured. Antonio D'Onofrio, a deformed hunchback, arose from his knees in the confessional completely cured. Pasquale Urbano of Foggia was able to discard his crutches; a woman regained her hearing after being completely deaf; and Francesco Ricciardi was cured of cancer of the stomach.

One of the best documented cures took place in 1949. Giovanni Savino, a construction worker and a member of the Franciscan Third Order, had placed a charge of dynamite under a huge boulder at the construction site. It did not go off, and after some minutes Giovanni went to check on it, but as soon as he got to the boulder, the charge detonated. Among his other serious injuries, the attendants noted that the right eye was gone completely, the socket was empty, and the other eye was badly damaged. Shortly after midnight on February 25, Giovanni woke up and smelled the aroma of roses and felt a gentle tap on his right cheek. Later that morning the ophthalmologist came to examine the injured left eye. When all the bandages were removed the doctors were amazed to see that Giovanni's face was completely healed, covered with new skin, and Giovanni said excitedly: "I can see you!"

"Turn your head this way," said the doctor, "so you can see me with your left eye."

"No," said Giovanni, "I see you with my right eye; I can't see anything out of my left eye."

Giovanni never did regain sight in his left eye, but what had happened was that what had previously been an empty socket, now contained a new right eye!

When these remarkable events were publicized, they attracted great numbers of pilgrims to San Giovanni Rotondo. Very frequently they were the occasion for complete spiritual conversions and a radical change of life. Many of the pilgrims also desired to have Padre Pio as their spiritual director, but he would accept only those who were willing to become persons of prayer, to carry their cross with full submission to God's will, to be faithful to the duties of their state in life, and to strive for Christian perfection. "I accept you quite willingly," he would say, "but on the condition that you always conduct yourself well, that you don't make a spectacle of me before God and men, and that you give good example of Christian living. Otherwise, I know how to use the whip." He once wrote to Antonietta Pompilio:

> I have made a pact with the Lord: when my soul has been purified in the flames of purgatory and deemed worthy to be admitted to the presence of God, I will take my place at the gate to paradise, but I shall not enter until I have seen the last of my spiritual children enter.

Of course, there were also some individuals who went to San Giovanni Rotondo for other purposes. Some of them were fanatical in their adulation of the Capuchin friar and others were motivated entirely by curiosity. These attitudes and exhibitions were distasteful to Padre Pio. They wanted to see him, to touch him, or even to cut off pieces of his Franciscan habit. In their attempts to touch him or jostle him, they increased greatly the pain of the stigmata. They were seeking the charismatic and the miraculous, sometimes forgetting that it is God who works miracles. On one occasion he showed a confrere the cuts in his

Franciscan cord and habit: "Look what they do! This is paganism! I have to be harsh with them. I don't like to do it, but if I don't act harshly, they will kill me!"

Eventually the mob scenes at San Giovanni Rotondo reached the point at which once again the Church authorities had to intervene.

29

THE LAST TRIAL

*T*HE CHURCH AUTHORITIES HAD NEVER taken their eyes off San Giovanni Rotondo. On December 31, 1951, two prelates were sent from the Holy Office: Bishop Giovanni Pepe and Abbot Emanuele Caronti. On January 16, 1952, the Minister General of the Capuchins sent Padre Agostino of Genoa as visitator, and on May 3, 1952, he had urged all the religious not to promote pilgrimages and not to distribute writings and photos of Padre Pio. On July 6, 1952, Padre Benigno of Sant'Ilario Milanese became Minister General of the Capuchin Order.

On April 14, 1960, Padre Clemente of Milwaukee was Minister General of the Capuchins and he wrote a letter to the Holy Father in which he described a serious and dangerous situation which had to be taken care of because of the problems that had arisen regarding the hospital work at the *Casa Sollievo della Sofferenza.* He requested an apostolic visitation "as soon as possible" as the only possibility for an effective and complete solution.

On July 22, 1960, the Holy Office named Bishop Carlo Maccari of the Sacred Congregation of the Council as visitator of San Giovanni Rotondo and the *Casa Sollievo della Sofferenza.* The visitator began his work on July 30, 1960, with a severe restriction on the admission of pilgrims into the church. He had noted, in fact, that some pilgrims, to get a place as close as possible to the altar where Padre Pio was celebrating Mass, were causing a disturbance with their uncontrolled outbursts and chaotic behavior. The same thing was true of the little church annexed to the monastery, where Padre Pio's confessional was located. In fact, the visitator ordered that the passage to the monastery church be closed with two gates. In the minds of the faithful, the gates were looked upon as the bars of a prison, and soon the papers were picturing Padre Pio as a persecuted victim and his superiors as tyrants.

The apostolic visitation came to an end on September 17, 1960, and the very next day the new superior arrived: Padre Rosario, formerly provincial of the Capuchins at Palermo. The apostolic visitator had removed the former superior, Padre Emilio, and had him transferred. Several other friars, including Padre Raffaele, were also transferred out of San Giovanni Rotondo.

On January 31, 1961, Cardinal Alfredo Ottaviani, Prefect of the Holy Office, sent a long, official document to Padre Rosario, containing a list of stipulations and restrictions. For the most part they were intended to stop any activities that might have the character of a cult directed towards the person of Padre Pio. It was forbidden for priests or bishops to serve at Padre Pio's Mass; women were not to confer with Padre Pio as he entered or left the confessional, and he was absolutely forbidden to speak with women alone anywhere; he was to celebrate his daily Mass at various hours; a safe distance was to be observed by lay people from Padre Pio's confessional; his Mass was to be completed in 40 minutes as a maximum; finally, he was to return to full religious observance.

Padre Pio accepted and obeyed the new restrictions with heroic resignation. "What can I do?", he said to a confrere. "I only pray that God will take me soon and free me from all this trouble."

One evening it was discovered that someone within the Capuchin community had bugged the places where Padre Pio normally conversed with people and this included his confessional! When the Padre heard of this, he was aghast: "My own brethren are doing this to me!" Actually, some have said that it was the former superior, Padre Emilio, who did it in order to put an end to the shocking rumor going around that Padre Pio was guilty of sexual relations with some of the women who came to him for direction.

Now he was deprived of everything, even the company of his dear friend Padre Raffaele. The only consolation and comfort he had was to place himself in the care of the Madonna. With her maternal assistance, he was able to proceed to the final stations of his *Via Crucis*.

30

AN ANGEL ON EARTH

*F*OR ALL HIS EXTRAORDINARY SPIRITUAL gifts and the fact that many considered him an "angel on earth," Padre Pio always remained incredibly human. He lived on the level of the supernatural, but he was to all appearances an ordinary Capuchin friar. All the basic psychological elements and faculties were there: intelligence, sensitivity, will, affectivity, a great capacity for love, ability to work and to suffer. The solidarity of his personality reflects the characteristics of the region in which he was born, but later it was modified by the rocky, barren land of San Giovanni Rotondo, which is like a limbo. His family background likewise exerted a powerful influence on his temperament, which naturally tended to have a reflective bent. The social environment was agricultural, humble, modest, bound to tradition, but also one that demanded work, sacrifice and renunciation, a holy fear of the Lord. But there was also good humor and the practice of prayer.

As a boy, his powers of observation, coupled with an uncommon sensitivity, gave him a precocious maturity. His desire to draw apart was not an antisocial reaction but an impelling need to nourish with the practice of prayer that vigorous seedling of religiosity that was growing in him more and more. This made him appear to be always occupied; he did not want to waste time.

The interior torment he experienced before he made his decisive response to God's call, his distancing himself from his mother and others who were dear to him, his novitiate and the years of formation in the Capuchin observances: all of these things contributed to the formation of his character. Always prompt in obedience, he nevertheless insisted on his right to life when the provincial wanted him, in spite of his state of health, to return to life in the monastery. Inclined as he was to sacrifice, he did not renounce as much as he could have. During his military service, he did not hesitate to ask for the intervention of persons in authority so that he could get exemptions on the basis of health. He also knew how to practice the "art of diplomacy." He was able to ask pardon if involuntarily, through lack of politeness or a hasty reaction, he wounded the feelings of a confrere. He was touched by any mark of courtesy or if he knew that someone was praying for him. He was also capable of treating others with utmost delicacy.

Padre Gerardo, who ultimately became the vice postulator of his cause for canonization, has written the following testimony:

> October 16 was my feast day and, as usual, I had gone to my office to work. I had not yet seen the Padre and consequently I eagerly awaited 11:00 a.m. to greet him. That particular morning I did not hear his cadenced and shuffling footsteps, accompanied by his coughing. I was continuing with my work when suddenly I had the feeling that someone had stopped at my door and had knocked very lightly. Curious, I got up and opened the door. He was standing there, smiling and a little embarrassed, like a child caught by its mother in the midst of some peccadillo. "Happy feast day!" he said, and taking it out of the key hole where he had inserted it, he handed me a little flower…

Padre Pio lived with his heart and for that reason he lived badly because, as he said, he had to "die at every moment from a death that does not cause death" (*Epistolario*, I, 1247s). For him, to live is to die and to die is to live. In fact , he once said: "I suffer when I do not suffer." And we have already seen that he suffered greatly from the wounds of the stigmata. He loved to suffer because of the spiritual benefits derived from suffering, but he was also able to say: "I can bear no more!" This was especially the case when he was betrayed and abandoned by all. Also, he sought relief from the heat of summer, but in the winter he was never able to get warm.

Although he spent all his time working and praying, he was also interested in social problems, politics, current events and art. He enjoyed the recitals that were held in the parlor of the friary as fundraisers for the *Casa Sollievo della Sofferenza*.

Padre Pio needed affection, friendship and the company of others. When a confrere got up to leave after a visit, Padre Pio would ask him to stay for a while longer, or he would say: "Come to visit me more often."

He liked to take part in the community recreation. In conversation he was affable, jovial and vivacious. He became famous in the community for his witticisms and his marvelous ability to mimic. It made him very happy to be able to provoke laughter and hilarity among those who listened to him. It seemed impossible to think of a man with so much physical and spiritual suffering, as being able to amuse and entertain his confreres with innocent jokes and humorous anecdotes that brought such happiness and good humor.

31

THE DECLINING YEARS

*T*HE PUBLICITY GIVEN TO THE APOSTOLIC visitation of Bishop Maccari served to diffuse ever more widely the fame of Padre Pio. People from all walks of life travelled to San Giovanni Rotondo, including cardinals and bishops who were in Rome for the Second Vatican Council. All of them were greatly edified by the humble Capuchin friar who bore the marks of the crucifixion. A great number of the ecclesiastical prelates asked for his prayers. Among the visitors was Cardinal Karol Wojtyla, Archbishop of Krakow and the future Pope John Paul II. He had already met Padre Pio as a seminarian in Rome from 1946 to 1948 and he had been greatly impressed by Padre Pio's spirituality. This time, however, on November 17, 1962, he left the following letter, written in Latin:

> Venerable Padre: I ask you to say a prayer for a mother of four young girls who is forty years old and lives in Krakow, Poland. During the last war she spent five years in a concentration camp in Germany and now finds herself in very great danger to her health and indeed to her life, on account of cancer. Pray that God, through the intercession of the Blessed Virgin, will have mercy on her and her family. Most gratefully in Christ.
>
> † Carolus Wojtyla
> Roma, Pontificio Collegio Polacco

The woman in question was Doctor Wanda Poltawska, collaborator and friend of the family of the Archbishop of Krakow. The letter was delivered by Bishop Andrea Deskur to Angelo Battisti, who in turn delivered it to Padre Pio. And when he read the letter, Padre Pio remarked: "To this we cannot say no!"

Ten days later, Bishop Deskur delivered another letter to Angelo Battisti. This letter was also written by Cardinal Wojtyla and again it was in Latin.

> Venerable Padre: The woman from Krakow, Poland, mother of four young girls, as she was about to undergo surgery, was suddenly cured. Thanking God and also you, venerable Padre, I offer my most heartfelt gratitude in the name of this woman, her husband and all her family. In Christ.
>
> † Carolus Wojtyla
> Roma, November 28, 1962

Padre Pio continued his ministry at full speed, although some time ago he had entered upon the period of decline. Physical and spiritual suffering had taken their toll. His eyesight had failed to such an extent that he had received permission to replace the daily recitation of the Divine Office with the fifteen decades of the rosary. Paul VI wanted him to be assured of complete freedom and tranquillity in his ministry and suggested that the superiors should deal with Padre Pio as if he were not bound by the vow of obedience. In 1966 Padre Pio felt that his end was near. He told his niece, Pia Forgione Pennelli: "In two years I shall no longer be with you."

Sometimes his spiritual daughters would ask him: "Father, how are you?" He would answer: "Bad, bad, bad! I can say: *Cursum consummavi, fidem servavi.* [I have finished the race, I have kept the faith. (2 Timothy 4:7)] I'm lacking only one thing: the grave."

He was approaching the jubilee anniversary of his crucifixion. Now he preferred to live in silence, fixing his eyes on an invisible presence, with his lips moving in prayer. He spoke little and he heard very few confessions. He tended to answer in monosyllables. He was preparing for his greatly desired meeting with the Lord. He was living without living! He was living by dying.

Lacking strength, he had to depend on the charity of his confreres to assist him in all his needs, both bodily and priestly. He had drunk to the last drop from the chalice of mortification. He had tasted the bitterness of suffering and was ready to die of love.

September 20, 1968, was the fiftieth anniversary of his stigmatization. There was no public celebration in the church. His spiritual sons and daughters surrounded him with affection, but he took little notice. There was no festivity; instead, he spent his time in prayer. The only outward sign was that the altar was covered with red roses. Many persons attended the Mass, and that evening the Rosary Square beneath the window of Padre Pio's cell was ablaze with lighted candles in the hands of his friends and spiritual sons and daughters.

The next day, due to an attack of asthma, he could not celebrate Mass. He received Communion, however, and afterwards he said: "It is finished! It is finished!"

His confreres did not pay any attention, because on other occasions he had been so low that he seemed to be at death's door, but he revived and resumed his work, stronger than before. Indeed, on that very afternoon he was able to give his blessing to the people who had gathered for the Fourth International Congress of Prayer Groups, scheduled to open the following day.

The superior tried to encourage Padre Pio by telling him that he would have to be in good form the following day for the sake of his spiritual sons and daughters. The Padre replied: "Another feast! I feel so confused that I ought to run away and disappear."

Sunday, September 22, was a special day. The superior asked Padre Pio to celebrate a sung Mass at five o'clock in the morning. Present at the Mass were 740 prayer groups. Padre Pio summoned all his strength and obeyed the superior's request. Assisted by Padre Onorato and Padre Valentino, he advanced to the altar and looked with astonishment at the crowds that filled the church. With a weak and tremulous voice he began the Mass. Then, raising his eyes to the mosaic of the Madonna, he said: "Madre, behold your children!" and broke into tears.

At the consecration of the Mass someone noticed that his hands were all white and clear, like the hands of a baby. The marks of the stigmata, which he had borne for fifty years, had disappeared. His mission was reaching its end.

At the end of the Mass, he intoned the *Ite, missa est.* He felt as if his heart would burst as the throng of people in the church gave him an ovation. Suddenly he began to fall backwards and a gasp went up from the crowd. If Fra Guglielmo had not been there to catch him, he would have suffered a heavy fall on the steps of the altar. The friars put him in a wheelchair to take him into the sacristy. As they wheeled him out, he gazed at the people and raised his arm and, with a catch in his voice, said: "My children! My children!" An impulse of love went out from him to the people. Torn with the desire to be united with God, he was distressed at the thought of leaving his spiritual children orphans. His sentiments were similar to those that Christ had experienced at the Last Supper.

After making his thanksgiving, he asked to be taken to his confessional. He passed through the crowds to reach it, but almost immediately he had to turn back. His countenance was white, he was trembling and confused, and his hands were cold. Meanwhile, in the church, the prayer groups were listening to the scheduled discourses. Padre Pio was supposed to give a welcoming talk at noon, but at 10:30 in the morning it was decided to do it earlier. So Padre Pio waved a white handkerchief from the window and gave his blessing to the people, who were delirious with joy and applause.

In the afternoon Padre Pio heard Mass, and at the end he tried to rise and give the people his blessing, but he couldn't stand. Later that evening he again wanted to give his blessing to the crowd. A voice rose above the din: "Padre, we love you!" Padre Pio could not keep back his tears. He stepped back from the window, for the last time.

32

IN THE ARMS
OF SISTER DEATH

$\mathcal{I}$N THE MIDDLE OF THE NIGHT PADRE Pellegrino went from door to door in the long corridor of the friary: "Wake up! Wake up! Padre Pio is dying!" It was two o'clock in the morning.

Padre Pellegrino was one of the assistants of Padre Pio and he had started his turn at 9:00 p.m. He is a privileged witness to the last earthly hours of Padre Pio:

> A little after 9:00 p.m. on September 22,1968, when Padre Mariano had already left cell No. 4 and I had entered, Padre Pio called me on the phone and asked me to come to his room. He was in bed, lying on his right side. He only asked me the time on the alarm clock on his bedside table. I wiped some tears from his reddened eyes and returned to room No. 4 to wait by the phone. Up until midnight Padre called me five or six times. His eyes were always red from weeping, but it was a peaceful, serene weeping.
>
> At midnight he said to me, like a frightened little child: "Stay with me, my son," and he frequently asked me what time it was. He looked at me with eyes full of supplication, and squeezed my hands tightly. Then, as if

he had forgotten about the time, he asked me: "Uaglio, have you said Mass?" I answered, smiling: "Father, it is too early now to say Mass." He replied: "Eh, this morning you will say Mass for me." And I said to him: "But every morning I say Mass for your intentions."

After a bit he wanted to go to confession, and when he had finished, he said: "My son, if the Lord calls me today, ask pardon for me from the confreres for all the bother I have given them and ask them and my spiritual children to pray for my soul."

I answered: "Padre, I am sure that the Lord will let you live for a long time yet, but if you are right, may I ask you for a final blessing for the brethren, for all your spiritual children and for all your sick?"

"Yes, I bless all, and ask the superior to give this last blessing in my name."

"And what shall I say to Pia, Ettoruccio and the family and to Sister Pia?"

"They all know how much I loved them," he said, his eyes filling with tears; "I bless them all; I bless them all."

Then he asked to renew his religious profession. At one o'clock he said to me: "Listen, my son, I can't breathe well in bed. Help me get up. I can breathe better in the chair."

He was accustomed to rising at one, two or three in the morning to prepare for the celebration of Mass, and before sitting in his chair, he would usually walk a few paces in the corridor. On this night I noticed, to my amazement, that he walked upright and rapidly, like a young man, so that it was not necessary for me to support him. As we approached the door to his cell, he said: "Let's go out on the balcony for a while."

I followed him, keeping a hand under his arm. He turned on the light, and when we reached the armchair, he sat down and looked around the balcony curiously. It seemed as if he were looking for something.

About five minutes later, he wanted to return to his cell. I tried to help him get up but he said: "I can't do it."

"Don't worry, Father," I said as I reached for the wheelchair, which was a few steps away. Then, holding him under the arms, I seated him on the chair. He lifted his feet and placed them on the footboard of the wheel-chair. In the cell, once he was situated in his easy chair, he signaled with his left hand as he looked at the wheelchair and he said: "Take it outside."

When I went back into the cell, I noticed that his face was very pallid and there was a cold sweat on his forehead. I became worried when I saw that his lips were turning blue. Meanwhile, he was repeating over and over in a voice that was weaker and weaker: "Jesus! Mary!"

I made a move to go to call a confrere, but he stopped me, saying: "Don't wake anyone." But I decided to do it anyway and when I had run a few paces, he called me again. I turned back, thinking he wanted something else, but when he repeated, "Don't wake anyone," I implored him: "Padre, let me do it," and I started out for the room of Padre Mariano. But seeing that Fra Guglielmo's door was open, I entered and turned on the light and said to him: "Padre Pio is dying." In a flash Fra Guglielmo was at Padre Pio's side and I raced to the telephone to call Doctor Sala. The doctor was there in ten minutes, and after one look at Padre Pio, he prepared an injection. When it was ready, Fra Guglielmo and I tried to lift the Padre but it was impossible, so the doctor administered the injection while Padre Pio was lying down. Then the doctor helped us put the Padre in his easy chair. During this time Padre Pio continued to murmur almost imperceptibly: "Jesus! Mary!"

Previously I had summoned the superior, Padre Mariano and the other friars, and they now began to arrive.

Doctor Giuseppe Sala now called Doctor Giovanni Scarale, the anaesthetist at the *Casa Sollievo della Sofferenza*. He quickly grasped the situation and suggested that the respiratory equipment be brought in immediately, in case it was necessary to use mechanical respiratory support. In the meantime, he inserted a nasal tube that was connected with an oxygen tank. He then called Doctor Gusso, the director of the clinic at the *Casa*.

Padre Pio was seated in the easy chair with his eyes closed and his head bent slightly forward. His breathing was labored and there was a light rattle in his throat. Padre Carmelo, the superior, felt Padre Pio's right hand. It was cold! He called him several times: "Padre! Padre!" There was no response, so the superior went to call Padre Raffaele, hoping that he would know what to do in this emergency.

In the meantime, Doctor Scarale removed the tube from Padre Pio's nose and replaced it with the face mask connected with the oxygen tank. Telling Padre Pio to breathe deeply, the doctor checked his pulse. But Padre Pio was paying no attention to the doctor's words. He seemed to be out of touch with his surroundings and simply kept repeating in a weak voice: "Jesus! Mary! Jesus! Mary!"

The medical attention lasted about ten minutes and during that time Padre Paolo, the sacristan, administered the sacrament of the sick. The superior, Padre Raffaele and Padre Mariano responded to the prayers. Suddenly Doctor Sala exclaimed: "He has a pulse! The pulse is returning!" but it was a false alarm. It died down completely, and Padre Pio gently rested his head against Doctor Scarale's left forearm and, without a sound, expired.

The doctors laid the corpse of Padre Pio on the bed. He had actually wanted to die in his armchair, where he had prayed, given comfort and counsel to so many friars and so many spiritual sons. He had wanted to die at his post, with the rosary in his hand, and calling upon Jesus and Mary. Doctor Giuseppe Gusso commented that the clinical signs of death were the most peaceful and sweet he had ever seen.

The superior asked all to leave so that the body of Padre Pio could be prepared for the wake and funeral. Checking the wounds of the stigmata, they were surprised to see that the wounds in the hands, feet and side were completely healed.

There was not the slightest trace of the stigmata. The skin was smooth and elastic. Photos were taken of the remarkable change, because for those who lived in close contact with Padre Pio, it was another mysterious phenomenon.

Several months ago it had been noticed that the flow of blood from the wounds was much less than previously. The friar who attended him had noted that the blood on the cloth covering his side was much lighter in color and those who kissed his hand had seen no scabs or dried blood on the back of his hands. When Doctor Sala was asked about the absence of any scar tissue where the wounds had been, he said that clinically it was unexplainable and would have to be characterized as preternatural. Later he wrote the following report:

> The hands, feet, thorax and other parts of the body of Padre Pio did not show any traces of wounds. No scars were present on either side of the hands and feet, nor on the side, where during his life wounds had been clearly visible. The skin in those areas of the body was exactly the same as in other parts of the body: soft, smooth and elastic, and digital pressure did not reveal any collapse of bone structure. The color and consistency did not give any sign of incision, laceration, wounds, cuts or inflammation. In conclusion, the palm and back of the hands, the instep and bottom of the feet, and the right side all had normal and integral skin of the same color as the rest of the body.

Various explanations were offered for the lack of any sign of the wounds of the stigmata which he had borne for many years:

— Padre Pio has completed his mission and perhaps the Lord has heard his prayer that the signs of the stigmata be hidden from the gaze of others;
— the supernatural gifts cannot undergo the natural decomposition of the body;
— the wounds of the stigmata were the means by which

Padre Pio shared in the sufferings of Christ, but after his death the stigmata would have no meaning.

Several years later, on May 25, 1971, Cardinal Corrado Ursi, Archbishop of Naples, preached the homily at the solemn inauguration of the *Via Crucis* at San Giovanni Rotondo. He commented as follows on the stigmata of Padre Pio:

> Padre Pio has borne wounds on his body, like Christ, to destroy the evils and sufferings of the contemporary world, but immediately after his death, his flesh became sound and healthy where it had been mysteriously wounded, and precisely to prove the certitude of the physical resurrection, the renewal of humanity, which occurred in him to some extent, and to show the credentials of the special mission he had received from God for the good of his brethren.

The superior decided to leave the hands and feet of Padre Pio covered with gloves and with stockings, not to hide the truth, but because at that moment it was not prudent to make public the new phenomenon, which could easily lend itself to hasty judgments. Everyone would have been asking for explanations which it was not possible to give under those circumstances.

Padre Pio looked serene and beautiful in death. Around his neck was the stole of the priesthood; in his hands were the crucifix, the rosary and the Rule of St. Francis. He could have died on the altar when he almost fell backwards at the end of his anniversary Mass, but perhaps God wanted him to enjoy the celebration and to be able to greet his spiritual children on that occasion.

His body was laid out in a wooden coffin. The procession to the church from the friary was made up of Capuchin friars, relatives and friends, all carrying lighted candles and chanting the *Miserere*. The coffin was carried to the sanctuary of the church and placed on a catafalque draped in black, surrounded by four lighted candles and two large bouquets of white flowers. At 8:30

the first suffrage Mass began with ten concelebrants. The church was packed with people, weeping and praying. From the top of the *Casa Sollievo della Sofferenza* the flag was at half mast. The whole town was in mourning, as well as people throughout the world. Pope Paul VI celebrated a suffrage Mass for Padre Pio and the Vatican newspaper, *L'Osservatore Romano* carried the following announcement on September 23, 1968:

At 2:30 a.m. today, Monday, Padre Pio of Pietrelcina passed from this life in the friary at San Giovanni Rotondo. "A man of humility, prayer and penance." These are the words used by Bishop Andrea Cesarano, when Pope John asked him for some information about Padre Pio. At the time, Cesarano had been Archbishop of Manfredonia for more than 25 years and had followed the life and ministry of the Capuchin friar on practically a daily basis.

Padre Pio is known all over the world and people came to him from every direction, both believers and sceptics, attracted by the fame of his virtues.

There has also been talk of his extraordinary supernatural gifts and on this point the Church will make a pronouncement in due time. We can only say that Padre Pio has guided and brought back to the Lord numerous souls; he has reconciled with God men who have drifted away from the faith and the Christian life, some of whom perhaps were enemies and hostile to religion. His confessional was a tribunal of mercy and firmness. There were even some who were sent away without receiving absolution, but in the majority of those cases they were anxious to return and find peace and understanding, and thus a new phase of the spiritual life was opened for them.

On the mountainside there arose, through his initiative, the *Casa Sollievo della Sofferenza*, which was dedicated by Cardinal Lercaro on May 5, 1956, with the blessing of Pope Pius XII, who received in audience a few days later the outstanding men of science from all over the world who had taken part in the dedication and the scientific congress that accompanied it. The *Casa Sollievo* is a very modern institution that attracts and treats hundreds and hundreds of patients, both physically and spiritually, and places at their disposition the most up-to-date technology and equipment. For twelve years now it has performed this service in an area which had lacked proper medical assistance and the population was in special need.

At the end, Padre Pio was unable to walk and he was suffering from asthma and bronchitis. Worn out by penances, he still carried on his ministry, but he had been granted permission to celebrate Mass seated and he was taken to his confessional in a wheelchair because of his inability to stand on his feet, but he did not want to retire from his ministry or the duties of every priest as a channel of the graces and mercy of God. He constantly offered himself for the intentions of the Pope and especially for the conversion of sinners and peace in the world.

Yesterday in the evening Padre Pio had blessed the faithful from a window in the friary, as was his custom. Friday of last week was a very special day in his life, because thousands of the faithful were united in prayer, citizens of San Giovanni Rotondo and other faithful, to bring to a close a special gathering of his prayer groups.

In the afternoon the doors of the church were closed, to give a rest to the *carabinieri* and the security officers and also to replace the wooden coffin with one of steel and covered with glass to protect the remains but still leave them visible. Padre Pio would be buried in the recently completed crypt in the new church. On September 24 and 25 thousands of mourners paid their respects to the memory of Padre Pio. Some estimates of the number of people from all over the world were as high as 100,000.

On September 26, at 3:30 p.m., the funeral cortège proceeded from the church to the center of the city. It was made up of military personnel, clergy, friars, religious, medical students and numerous citizens and visitors. Overhead the helicopters of the Italian Air Force and the police dropped flowers and religious leaflets. Professor Enrico Medi was at the microphone, leading the rosary and offering a commentary. Among other things, this is what he said:

> A living crucifix for fifty years. His hands, his feet, his side bore the wounds of the Lord. His forehead, crowned with thorns, and his heart pierced by the sins of the world, like the heart of Jesus.
>
> In a certain sense, and it is especially true regarding his union with the Lord by participation, to see him was to see Jesus, as in every person redeemed by the precious blood of the Redeemer.
>
> And thus, there has been in the midst of us poor souls, someone we have scarcely noticed. We have seen in him suffering, graces and miracles. We have asked him for consolation and encouragement; we have listened to his words and counsel.
>
> But who has been able to penetrate that heart so consumed and so lacerated; which has fulfilled its mission to the very end, even to the last drop of blood?... He has not left us. This body of his will be a source of grace. I am only a poor layman. The authority of the Church will speak to us. We are obedient, disciplined and faithful sons of the authority of the Church, to the last breath of our hearts. But what is certain, may the Church allow me to say so, is that we do not pray for Padre Pio. But let us say: Padre Pio, pray for us!...
>
> Anyone who has known him and has watched him, has sometimes thought that he was rough, perhaps a bit too severe, that he treated people with a certain amount of harshness. It was his great humility that prevailed. That day, fifty years ago, when he received the stigmata, his humility was profoundly shaken. He wanted to cast himself into the abyss of nothingness, so that the stigmata could not be for him a source of comfort or consolation...

It seems to me that there has never been a saint in the life of the Church, in the history of the Church, from whom Christ has asked so much blood as from Padre Pio.

Saint Francis bore the stigmata for three years; Padre Pio, for fifty years! His was a permanent, long crucifixion… That continual and perennial passion: blood, blood, blood, to carry out his salvific, sanctifying mission to the very end.

At the end of his life he wanted to look again from the balcony at the plains of Foggia and the sea of Manfredonia. Perhaps he thought of the crowds that greeted him every afternoon at the *Angelus*. Then he retired to his cell. He began to collapse, to say *Jesus, Mary! Jesus, Mary!* And praying in a way so as not to disturb anyone, with that courtesy which the love of the saints and his own politeness dictates, he went to heaven.

In the city square Doctor Sala then read a salutation in honor of Padre Pio. The procession resumed, but it was more of a triumphal parade than a funeral procession. It was the city's homage to a great personage.

Back at the *piazza* in front of the Church, an outdoor Mass was celebrated at 7:00 p.m., with 24 priests concelebrating and the Minister General of the Capuchins as principal celebrant. The Apostolic Administrator for Foggia gave a stirring homily and then read a telegram from the Holy See:

The Supreme Pontiff has received with paternal sorrow the news of the pious passing of Padre Pio of Pietrelcina and as he prays that the Lord will grant his faithful servant the eternal crown of justice, he comforts the religious community, the doctors and staff of *Casa Sollievo della Sofferenza* and the entire population of San Giovanni Rotondo with a special apostolic blessing.

At the end of the Mass the Bishop of Manfredonia, Antonio Cunial, gave the final blessing to the deceased. Then the coffin was taken to the crypt of the church for burial and over the grave they placed a huge block of blue granite as a sarcophagus.

As early as 1923 Padre Pio had requested that his remains be buried in a quiet corner in the soil of the region. His wish was granted, even if the tranquillity was to last only one night. The very next day, throngs of people visited the tomb to pray and to experience his lingering presence.

33

PRELUDE TO GLORY

$\mathcal{O}$N NOVEMBER 4, 1969, A LITTLE MORE
than a year after the peaceful passing of Padre Pio from this life,
the Curia of the Capuchin Order forwarded to the apostolic administrator of the archdiocese of Manfredonia, Bishop Antonio
Cunial, the petition to open the process for the canonization of
Padre Pio. On November 23 Bishop Cunial informed the postulator general of the Capuchin Order that he had authorized
the collection of information that is required for the first phase
of the process. The Curia of the Capuchins then wrote to the
cardinals, archbishops and bishops of the world, asking that
letters be sent to the Pope for authorization to introduce the
cause.

All the prelates were asked for individual letters, but the
letter from Poland was a collective document, signed by the
Polish Conference of Bishops. The letter was dated May 3, 1972,
and it was signed by two cardinals and forty-three archbishops and bishops. Immediately after the signature of Cardinal
Wyszynski, Primate of Poland, was the signature of Cardinal
Wojtyla, Archbishop of Krakow and future Pope John Paul II.
The petition from the Polish bishops reads as follows:

> Most Holy Father: Padre Pio of Pietrelcina, professed
> priest of the Order of Friars Minor Capuchin, can be listed

among the men consecrated to God who, outstanding in virtue, have died with the reputation of sanctity. Some of us have seen with our own eyes Padre Pio and his apostolate; others have been informed by those who have seen, heard and written about him; all of us are convinced of the holiness of life and the special mission of this man of the Church. This has been demonstrated by his long exemplary life; his pattern of virtues; and especially his constant prayer, with special devotion to the Passion of our Lord Jesus Christ and to the Blessed Virgin Mary; by his various heroic sacrifices and penance; by his marvelous apostolate, permeated with love of God and of neighbor. This long exemplary life is well known throughout the Christian world, and also in our country. The proof of his reputation for sanctity can be found in his works. The *Casa Sollievo della Sofferenza* and the prayer groups, which are constantly expanding and producing many fruits of a religious and social nature; and the many and diverse graces which the faithful attribute to his intercession.

At a time in which so many things that are not true or right are proclaimed about religious life, about the apostolate of religious, of the dignity and duties of priests, the person of Padre Pio, a religious and a priest who is a contemporary, with his mode of life and his activities, offers to the restless world an excellent and desirable example of a man full of God...

The Second Vatican Council asks that religious have an apostolate which they are required to promote especially by prayer and penance in their life. The same Council asks that religious priests be providential collaborators with the episcopal order, given the increasing needs of souls.

All of these things are clearly demonstrated in Padre Pio, a man who is the personification of prayer and a man of indescribable sacrifices for sinners, sacrifices which come from a correct understanding of the priestly office of cooperating with Christ in the work of redemption, filling up in his own flesh what is wanting to the sufferings of Christ, for the benefit of the Body of Him who is the Church (Col 1:24).

Keeping all this in mind and considering his reputation for sanctity, which exists also in Poland and continues and is manifested especially in the prayers which the faithful address to God to obtain various graces through the intercession of Padre Pio, we have deemed it opportune to ask Your Holiness that you deign to introduce the Cause for Beatification and Canonization of this Servant of God, for the greater glory of God and the good of Holy Church.

On January 16, 1973, the new archbishop of Manfredonia, Valentino Vailati, sent to the Congregation for the Causes of Saints the documentation required for introducing the cause of Padre Pio. The Congregation judged the documentation to be insufficient and the process was slowed down considerably. Later, in 1974, Paul VI entrusted to Cardinal Wojtyla of Krakow a special assignment. Accompanied by seven Polish priests, the Cardinal went to San Giovanni Rotondo to celebrate Mass in the crypt. In his homily he said: "Particularly moving and especially profound is the fact that we are celebrating this Eucharist near the tomb of Padre Pio, who preached the passion and resurrection of Jesus Christ by means of his entire life."

The next day he celebrated Mass in the little church adjacent to the friary and said: "This ancient church is the place where I first met the Servant of God, Padre Pio. And after almost twenty-seven years I have before my eyes his person, his presence, his words, the Mass celebrated by him at a side altar, and then this confessional, where he heard the confessions of women."

Then, in keeping with the theme of that day's liturgy, "The living man is the glory of God," he added. "After almost twenty-seven years I see this truth, which is proclaimed in the liturgy, made incarnate in Padre Pio: *Padre Pio is the glory of the living God.*"

The Capuchin provincials were convinced of the holiness of life of their confrere, a life of sacrifice and penance. All things considered, he was an exemplary religious and a model priest, totally dedicated to doing good for others, especially in the ministry of the confessional and in spiritual direction. Consequently, they considered it opportune to petition the Holy Father to authorize the introduction of the process of canonization of the Servant of God, Padre Pio of Pietrelcina, for the greater glory of God and the good of the Church. When the Capuchin Order held a General Chapter in Rome, it sent the Holy Father a formal petition on July 9, 1982.

The Holy Father was well aware of the reputation for sanctity enjoyed by Padre Pio, so he passed along the request to the Congregation for the Causes of Saints. On October 23 the Congregation handed down a favorable response for the opening of the cause. When the Prefect of the Congregation, Cardinal Pietro Palazzini, presented the documentation to John Paul II on November 29, 1982, it was approved and confirmed on the very same day.

The ecclesiastical tribunal convened with appropriate solemnity at San Giovanni Rotondo on March 20, 1983, to start the official investigation into the life and virtues of the Servant of God, Padre Pio of Pietrelcina. The first of 74 invited witnesses was heard on April 7, 1983, and the investigation extended over a period of seven years. At the same time the historical commission was busy collecting and cataloguing all pertinent documents and records. The work of the tribunal was concluded with a solemn ceremony at San Giovanni Rotondo on January 21, 1990, and a total of 104 volumes were turned over to the Congregation for the Causes of Saints on February 13, 1990. On December 3, 1990, the Congregation named Padre Cristoforo Bove, OFM Conv., official *relator* of the cause.

The second phase of the process began with the publication of the procedural acts and the opening of the investigation into the candidate's "heroic virtues." The affirmative verdict concerning Padre Pio's heroic virtue was passed at a plenary session of the Congregation on June 3, 1997, and approved at a special congress of theological consultants on October 21 of the same year. Pope John Paul II convalidated the decision of these two groups by conferring on Padre Pio the title "Venerable," on December 18, 1997.

CONGREGATION FOR THE CAUSES OF SAINTS
DECREE ON THE VIRTUES OF PADRE PIO OF PIETRELCINA

"May I never boast of anything but the cross of our Lord Jesus Christ!" (Gal 6:14).

Like the Apostle Paul, Padre Pio of Pietrelcina placed at the apex of his life and his apostolate the Holy Cross, which was his strength, his wisdom and his glory. Freed from the vanity of the world and burning with love for Jesus Christ, he conformed himself to Christ in the immolation of self for the salvation of the world. He was so perfect in the following and imitation of the Divine Victim, that he could say: "I have been crucified with Christ, and the life I live now is not my own; Christ is living in me" (Gal 2:19-20). He did not want for himself the treasures of grace that God showered upon him with singular generosity; therefore in his sacred ministry he unceasingly served the men and women who came to him and he generated an immense multitude of spiritual sons and daughters.

This most worthy follower of St. Francis of Assisi was born on May 25, 1887, at Pietrelcina, in the archdiocese of Benevento, to Grazio Forgione and Maria Giuseppa Di Nunzio. He was baptized the following day with the name Francesco. He passed his infancy and adolescence in a serene and tranquil environment: home, church, the farmland, and later the school. At the age of 12 he received the sacrament of Confirmation and Holy Communion.

At the age of 16, on January 6, 1903, he entered the novitiate of the Friars Minor Capuchin at Morcone where, on January 22, he was clothed in the Franciscan habit and given the name Fra Pio. Successfully completing the year of novitiate, he made profession of simple vows and, on January 27, 1907, profession of solemn vows.

After ordination to the priesthood, on August 10, 1910, at Benevento, he remained with his family until 1916 for reasons of health. In September of that same year he was sent to the friary at San Giovanni Rotondo, and there he remained until his death, to the edification of many of the faithful. In 1918 they saw in him the marks of the Passion of the Lord and other charisms.

Burning with love of God and love of neighbor, Padre Pio lived to the full his vocation to contribute to the redemption of man in accordance with the special mission that characterized his entire life. He carried out this program by using three means: the direction of souls, reconciliation through the sacrament of penance, celebration of Mass. The highest moment in his apostolic activity was the celebration of Mass. The faithful who participated perceived that this constituted the apex and the plenitude of his spirituality.

On the social level, Padre Pio exerted himself strenuously to alleviate the sorrows and miseries of numerous families, especially by founding the *Casa Sollievo della Sofferenza*, which was inaugurated on May 5, 1956. On the spiritual level he founded the prayer groups, which he himself described as "reservoirs of faith and... furnaces of love," and the Sovereign Pontiff had described as "a great river of persons who pray."

For the Servant of God his faith was his life; everything he desired and everything he did was in the light of that faith. In order to nourish his faith, he was assiduously dedicated to the practice of prayer. The day and a good part of the night were, in fact, spent in colloquium with God. He once said: "In books we search for God; in prayer we find him. Prayer is the key that opens the heart to God." Faith led him always to the acceptance of the mysterious will of God. He was a religious immersed in the supernatural reality and he permeated everything with his faith, which touched all who came into contact with him.

Not only was he a man of hope and complete trust in God, but he instilled these virtues in souls by word and example.

He was filled with the love of God, fulfilling his every expectation; charity was the dominant impulse in his daily life: to love God and to make him loved. His principal preoccupation: to grow in charity and to make it grow in others. This was the secret of his life of sacrifice, which was spent in the confessional and in the direction of souls.

He manifested the intensity of his love of neighbor by receiving for more than fifty years the numerous persons who were recipients of his sacred ministry, his counsel and his comfort. He was a veritable magnet of love; they sought him in the church, in the sacristy and in the friary. And he gave his love to all, revitalizing their faith, distributing graces, bringing evangelical light and comfort. In the poor, the sick and the suffering, he saw the image of Christ and he gave himself especially for them.

He practiced the virtue of prudence in an exemplary way, acting and counseling in accordance with God's light.

His interest was the glory of God and the good of souls. He treated them all without any preference, but with honesty and great respect.

The virtue of fortitude was resplendent in him. He understood very early that his path would be that of the Cross, and he accepted it immediately with courage and love. For many years he experienced spiritual sufferings. For years he bore the sufferings of his wounds with admirable fortitude. In silence and in prayer he accepted interventions of ecclesiastical authority and those of his Order. In the face of calumny, he remained silent.

Prayer and mortification were the means he used habitually to practice the virtue of temperance in conformity with Franciscan spirituality. He was temperate in his thinking and in his manner of life.

Aware of the obligation assumed in the consecrated life, he generously fulfilled the religious vows. He loved them because they were the counsels given by Christ and because they were the means of perfection.

He was obedient in all things to the commands of his superiors, even when they were burdensome. His obedience was supernatural in intention, universal in its extension, and integral in its execution.

He lived the spirit of poverty with complete detachment from self, from created goods, from personal comfort, and from honors.

He always had a special love for the virtue of chastity. His behavior was always modest in every respect and with everybody.

He sincerely considered himself to be useless, unworthy of the gifts received from God, full of miseries and at the same time of divine favors. In the midst of great admiration from the world, he would say: "I want to be only a poor friar who prays."

Throughout his youth his health was always delicate, and in the latter years his health declined rapidly.

Sister Death took him, well prepared and serene, on September 23, 1968, at the age of 81. His funeral was attended by an extraordinarily large concourse of people.

On February 20, 1971, scarcely three years after the death of the Servant of God, Paul VI told the superiors of the Capuchin Order: "See what fame he had and what a worldwide clientele he had gathered around himself! But why? Perhaps because he was a philosopher? Because he was a wise man? Because he had means at his disposal? Because he celebrated Mass with great humility, heard confessions from dawn to dusk, and was a representative stamped with the stigmata of our Lord. He was a man of prayer and of suffering."

During his lifetime he already enjoyed a reputation for holiness, because of his virtues, his spirit of prayer, his sacrifice and total dedication for the good of souls.

In the years leading to his death, his reputation for sanctity and miracles constantly increased more and more. It became an ecclesial phenomenon spread throughout the world and touching every class of persons.

Thus God has manifested in the Church his will to glorify on earth his faithful Servant. Not much time passed before the Friars Minor Capuchin took the steps required by Canon Law to initiate the cause for beatification and canonization. Having examined every aspect of the case the Holy See, in accordance with the *Motu Proprio* "Sanctitas Clarior," granted the *nulla osta* on November 29, 1982.

The Archbishop of Manfredonia was able to proceed with the introduction of the Cause and the celebration of the cognitive process (1983-1990). On December 7, 1990, the Congregation for the Causes of Saints recognized its juridic validity. Finally, the *Positio* was discussed, as is the custom, as to whether the Servant of God had practiced the virtues to a heroic degree. On June 13, 1997, the Congress of Theological Consultors was held, resulting in a positive decision. On the following October 21, with Bishop Andrea Maria Erba as *Ponente della Causa,* the Cardinals and Bishops recognized that Padre Pio of Pietrelcina has practiced to a heroic degree the theological, cardinal and annexed virtues.

The undersigned Pro-Prefect has informed the Sovereign Pontiff, John Paul II, concerning the completed phases of the Cause. His Holiness, accepting and approving the judgment of the Congregation for the Causes of Saints, has ordained that the decree on the heroicity of the virtues of the Servant of God should be redacted.

That having been executed in accordance with the norms, on today's date, the Pro-Prefect, the *Ponente della Causa,* the Secretary Archbishop of the Congregation, and the other persons who are normally summoned, in their presence, the Most Holy Father has solemnly declared:

It is evident that the Servant of God, Padre Pio of Pietrelcina, in the world Francesco Forgione, professed priest of the Order of Friars Minor Capuchin, has practiced to a heroic degree the theological virtues of faith, hope and charity, towards God and towards neighbor, and also the cardinal virtues of prudence, justice, fortitude and temperance, and the annexed virtues.

The Supreme Pontiff has commanded that this Decree should be published and preserved in the acts of the Congregation for the Causes of the Saints.

Given at Rome, in the year of our Lord, December 18, 1997.

†Alberto Bovone
Titular Archbishop of Caesarea di Numidia
Pro-Prefect
†Edward Nowak
Titular Archbishop of Luni
Secretary

While the diocesan process was still in progress, His Holiness Pope John Paul II visited the region of Capitanata and stopped first of all at San Giovanni Rotondo. It was the first time that a Pope visited that holy sanctuary, together with fifty thousand pilgrims from all over the world. It was an historic event, an event without precedent. The date was May 23, 1987, and before the Holy Father went down to the crypt to pray at the tomb of Padre Pio, he addressed the assembled friars, clergy and faithful:

Great is my joy at this meeting, for various reasons. As you know, these places carry with them personal memories, memories of my visits to Padre Pio both during his earthly life and, after his death, to his tomb.

Moreover, it is always a delight for me to meet the children of St. Francis, whom I see in great numbers here today. I very much love Franciscan spirituality. One of my first apostolic journeys in Italy was to the tomb of the Seraphic Father in Assisi, and all of you surely recall the ecumenical day celebrated there in October of last year. Finally, I delight in finding myself in this church dedicated to Our Lady of Graces. This sacred place has certainly been the hub of a great spiritual radiation in recent times, thanks to the work of Padre Pio; but how has this work come about, if not through a continuous outpouring of grace which has descended, through Mary, upon the crowds that come here seeking peace and pardon?

Padre Pio was devoted to Our Lady, the Mother of priests, who has a special role in conforming them to the supreme model of her Son.

The desire to imitate Christ was particularly strong in Padre Pio. Docile to grace from his childhood, already at fifteen years of age he received from God the gift of seeing clearly his life's path. Recalling that period, he tells us: "The secure place, the refuge of peace, was in the ranks of the ecclesiastical militia. And where will I better be able to serve you, O Lord, than in the cloister and under the banner of the Poverello of Assisi?… May Jesus grant me the grace to be a less unworthy son of St. Francis, that I may be an example to my confreres."

We might say that the Lord heeded his request beyond his own expectations. In fact, as a religious he generously lived out the ideal of the Capuchin friars, just as he lived out *the ideal of the priest*. For this reason he offers even today a point of reference, because in him the two aspects that characterize the Catholic priesthood were particularly embraced and found a special spiritual resonance: the faculties *to consecrate the Body and Blood of the Lord* and *to remit sin*. Were not the altar and the confessional the two poles of his life? This priestly witness contains a message as valid as it is timely.

In this regard it is enough to recall what the Second Vatican Council teaches regarding the sacrament of the priesthood, especially in the Decree *Presbyterorum Ordinis*. It confirms those essential and perennial values of the priesthood which were realized in an excellent way in Padre Pio. Certainly it also proposes new perspectives and forms of witness more adapted to the mentality of our times. However, it would be a serious error if, due to a misguided push for renewal, the priests were to forget those fundamental values; one certainly cannot appeal to the Council to validate such an error.

An essential aspect of the sacred ministry, one which we find in the life of Padre Pio, is the priest's self-offering, in Christ and with Christ, as a *victim* of expiation and reparation for the sins of the people. The priest must ever have before his eyes the classic definition of his mission contained in the *Letter to the Hebrews:* "Every high priest chosen from among men is appointed to act on behalf of men in relation to God, to offer gifts and sacrifices for sins" (Heb 5:1). This definition is echoed by the Council, when it teaches that "priests as ministers of the sacred mysteries, especially in the sacrifice of the Mass, act in a special way in the person of Christ who gave himself as a victim to sanctify men" (*Presbyterorum Ordinis*, 13).

This offering must reach its fullest expression in the celebration of the Eucharistic sacrifice. Who does not recall the fervor with which Padre Pio relived the Passion of Christ in the Mass? Whence the esteem he had for the Mass — which he called "a tremendous mystery" — as the decisive moment of man's salvation and sanctification through participation in the very sufferings of Christ Crucified. "The whole of Calvary is in the Mass," he said. For him the Mass was the "fount and the culmination," the hub and the center of his whole life and work.

This intimate and loving participation in the Sacrifice of the Cross was the source of Padre Pio's dedication to and availability for souls, especially those tangled in the snares of sin and in the anxieties of human misery. This is so well known that I do not intend to dwell on it; but I wish only to highlight several points that seem important to me, because here, too, we find agreement between the conduct of Padre Pio and the teaching of the Council.

This humble religious received with docility the infusion of that "spirit of grace and counsel," of which the Council speaks, that spirit which is to enable the pastor of souls to "help and govern the people in a pure heart" (*Presbyterorum Ordinis,* 7).

He applied himself in a particular way — in accordance with another conciliar teaching (cf. *ibid.,* 9) — in *spiritual direction,* spending his energies in helping souls to discover and put to good use the gifts and charisms which God grants how and when he wishes in his mysterious generosity.

This, too, can be an example for many priests to resume or to improve a "service to their brethren" tied in this way to their specific mission, which has always been — and must be today as well — rich in spiritual fruits for the whole people of God, especially with respect to the promotion of holiness and of religious vocations.

If the characteristic element of the priesthood is the administration of the sacraments, this ministry will not succeed in being credible in the eyes of people if the priest does not at the same time satisfy the demands of *fraternal charity.* In this area, too, we know well what Padre Pio achieved, how lively was his sense of justice and mercy, his *compassion for those who suffered,* and how concretely he committed himself to helping them, with the assistance of competent and generous collaborators. "Into the depths of this soul," Padre Pio said of himself, "it seems to me that God has poured many graces of compassion for the miseries of others, especially with respect to the poor and needy... If I know, then, that a person is afflicted, whether in soul or body, what would I not do before the Lord in order to see him freed from his ills? Just to see him saved, I would gladly take on all his afflictions, yielding in his favor the fruits of this suffering, if the Lord would permit me."

I wish to thank the Lord with you for having given us dear Padre Pio, for having given him to our generation in this very tormented century. In his love for God and for his brethren he is a sign of great hope, and he invites all, especially us priests, not to leave him alone in this mission of charity.

May the Virgin of the Holy Rosary — to whom he was so devoted, and whom we venerate in a special way during this month dedicated to her — help us to be perfect imitators of the one Master, her Son Jesus.

These resounding words are a beautiful prelude to the ardently longed-for glorification of Padre Pio of Pietrelcina.

AN AFTERWORD

*A*N ESTIMATED 200,000 FAITHFUL gathered in St. Peter's Square and the Via della Conciliazione on Sunday, May 2, 1999, for the solemn Mass at which Pope John Paul II beatified Padre Pio of Pietrelcina, a humble Capuchin priest who often claimed that his sole desire in life was "to be a poor friar who prays." An additional 100,000 gathered in the square of St. John Lateran and followed the ceremony on large-screen televisions. In his homily based on the readings for the Fifth Sunday of Easter, the Holy Father stated that Padre Pio "shared in the Passion with a special intensity: the unique gifts which were given to him, and the interior and mystical sufferings which accompanied them, allowed him constantly to participate in the Lord's agonies, never wavering in his sense that 'Calvary is the hill of the saints.'" The Pope prayed that Blessed Padre Pio would look down from heaven and come to the help of all, bringing peace and consolation to every heart.

On Monday, May 3, 1999, the day after his beatification, the Holy Father addressed a large gathering of pilgrims who had come to Rome for the event. This is what he said to them:

> Divine Providence wanted Padre Pio to be beatified on the eve of the Great Jubilee of the Year 2000, as a dramatic century draws to a close. What is the message that the Lord would like to offer to believers and to all humanity with this event of major spiritual importance?

Padre Pio's witness, which is evident from his life and even from his physical condition, suggests to us that this message coincides with the essential meaning of the Jubilee now close at hand: Jesus is the one Savior of the world. In him God's mercy was made flesh in the fullness of time, to bring salvation to humanity mortally wounded by sin. "By his wounds you have been healed" (1 P 2:24), the blessed father repeated to all in the words of the Apostle Peter, he whose body was marked with those wounds.

In 60 years of religious life, practically all spent at San Giovanni Rotondo, he was totally dedicated to prayer and to the ministry of reconciliation and spiritual direction. This was well emphasized by the Servant of God, Pope Paul VI: "Look what fame he had... But why?... Because he said Mass humbly, heard confessions from dawn to dusk and was... the one who bore the wounds of our Lord. He was a man of prayer and suffering."

Totally absorbed in God, always bearing the marks of Jesus' Passion in his body, he was bread broken for men and women starving for God the Father's forgiveness. His stigmata, like those of Francis of Assisi, were the work and sign of divine mercy, which redeemed the world by the Cross of Jesus Christ. Those open, bleeding wounds spoke of God's love for everyone, especially for those sick in body and spirit.

And what can be said of his life, an endless spiritual combat, sustained by the weapons of prayer, centered on the sacred daily acts of Confession and Mass? Holy Mass was the heart of his whole day, the almost anxious concern of all his hours, his moment of closest communion with Jesus, Priest and Victim. He felt called to share in Christ's agony, an agony which continues until the end of the world.

Dear friends, in our time, when we are still under the illusion that conflicts can be resolved by violence and superior strength, and frequently give in to the temptation to abuse the force of arms, Padre Pio repeats what he once said: "What a dreadful thing war is! In every person wounded in the flesh, there is Jesus suffering." Nor should we fail to note that both his works — the "House for the Relief of Suffering" and the prayer groups — were conceived by him in 1940, as the catastrophe of the Second World War loomed in Europe. He was not idle, but from his secluded friary in Gargano, he responded with prayer, works of mercy and love, for God and neighbor. And today, from heaven, he is telling everyone again that this is the authentic way of peace.

The prayer groups and the "House for the Relief of Suffering": these are two significant "gifts" which Padre Pio has left us. Conceived and desired by him as a hospital for the sick poor, the "House for the Relief of Suffering" was planned from the start as a health-care facility open to everyone, but this was no reason for it to be less equipped than other hospitals. Indeed, Padre Pio wanted it to have the most advanced scientific and technological equipment, so that it would be a place of authentic hospitality, loving respect and effective treatment for every suffering person. Is it not a true miracle of Providence that it continues to grow in accordance with its founder's spirit?

As for the prayer groups, he wanted them to be like beacons of light and love in the world. He longed for many souls to join him in prayer: "Pray," he used to say, "pray to the Lord with me, because the whole world needs prayers. And every day, when your heart especially feels the loneliness of life, pray, pray to the Lord together, because God too needs our prayers!" It was his intention to create an army of praying people who would be a "leaven" in the world by the strength of prayer. And today the whole Church is grateful to him for this precious legacy, admires the holiness of her son and invites everyone to follow his example.

Dear brothers and sisters, Padre Pio's witness is a powerful call to the supernatural dimension, not to be confused with exaggerated concern for miracles, a deviation which he always and resolutely shunned.

Priests and consecrated persons in particular should look to him. He teaches priests to become the docile and generous instruments of divine grace, which heals people at the root of their ills, restoring peace of heart to them. The altar and the confessional were the two focal points of his life: the charismatic intensity with which he celebrated the divine mysteries is a very salutary witness, to shake priests from the temptation of habit and help them rediscover, day by day, the inexhaustible treasure of spiritual, moral and social renewal which is placed in their hands.

To consecrated persons and especially to the Franciscan family, he offers a witness of extraordinary fidelity. Francis was his baptismal name, and he was a worthy follower of the Seraphic Father in poverty, chastity and obedience from the time he first entered the friary. He practiced the Capuchin rule in all its rigor, generously embracing the life of penance. He found no gratification in pain but chose it as a way of expiation and purification. Like the Poor Man of Assisi, he aimed at conformity with Jesus Christ, desiring only "to love and to suffer," in order to help the Lord in the exhausting and demanding work of salvation. In "firm, constant and iron" obedience, he found the highest expression of his unconditional love for God and the Church.

What a consolation to feel we have Padre Pio close to us, one who only wanted to be "a poor friar who prays": a brother of Christ, a brother of Francis, a brother of the suffering, a brother of each one of us. May his help guide us on the way of the Gospel and make us ever more generous in following Christ!

May the Blessed Virgin Mary, whom he loved and helped others to love with profound devotion, obtain this for us. May his intercession, which we confidently invoke, obtain this for us.

I accompany these hopes with my Apostolic Blessing, which I cordially impart to you, dear pilgrims present here, and to all who are united in spirit with our festive gathering.

CHRONOLOGY

1887 May 25: born at Pietrelcina to Grazio Forgione and Maria Giuseppa Di Nunzio.

May 26: baptized with the name Francesco.

1892 At age of five, consecrates himself to God.

1899 At age of 11, receives First Communion.

September 27: receives sacrament of Confirmation.

1903 January 6: enters Capuchin novitiate at Morcone.

January 27: clothed in Capuchin habit with the name Fra Pio of Pietrelcina.

1904 January 22: profession of simple vows.

January 25: to Sant'Elia a Pianisi to complete liberal arts education.

1905 End of October: to San Marco la Catola for course in philosophy.

1906 End of April: returns to Sant'Elia a Pianisi to finish philosophy course.

1907 January 27: profession of solemn vows.

October 9-10: at San Marco la Catola for philosophy examination.

End of October: at Serracapriola to start study of theology.

1908 November: to Montefusco, continues study of theology.

December 19: to Benevento for minor orders.

December 21: ordained subdeacon.

1909 May: at Pietrelcina for reasons of health.

July 18: at Morcone, ordained deacon.

1910 August 10: at cathedral in Benevento, ordained priest.

1915 November 6: called for military service.

1916 February 17: at friary of Sant'Anna in Foggia.

July 28: first visit to San Giovanni Rotondo.

December 18: reports for military service in Naples.

December 30: on military leave for convalescence.

1917 May 16: accompanies his sister Graziella to Rome to enter Brigittines.

1918 March 5: resumes military service at Naples.

March 16: dismissed from military service because of double bronchial infection.

March 18: returns to San Giovanni Rotondo.

August 5-7: receives gift of mystical transverberation.

September 20: receives the stigmata.

1919 May 15-16: sees Professor Luigi Romanelli.

July 26: sees Professor Amico Bignami.

October 8: sees Doctor Giorgio Festa.

1923 June 17: forbidden to celebrate public Masses.

June 26: permitted to celebrate Mass in the church.

August 8: notified of possible transfer from San Giovanni Rotondo.

1925 October 5: has surgery without general anaesthesia.

1929 January 3: death of Mamma Peppa.

1931 June 9: again ordered to celebrate Mass privately.

1933 July 16: permission to celebrate Mass in public.

1934 March 25: permission to hear confessions of men.

May 12: permission to hear women's confessions.

1946 October 7: death of his father, Grazio Forgione.

1947 May 19: starts construction of *Casa Sollievo della Sofferenza.*

1956 May 5: dedication of the hospital.

July 2: lays cornerstone of new church.

1959 July 1: consecration of new church, *Santa Maria delle Grazie.*

August 5-6: statue of Our Lady of Fatima at San Giovanni Rotondo.

1960 July 30: Bishop Carlo Maccari, apostolic visitator arrives.

1968 September 22: celebrates his last Mass.

September 23: death of Padre Pio.

September 26: solemn funeral.

1969 November 4: the postulator general of the Capuchins asks the apostolic administrator, Bishop Antonio Cunial, to initiate discussion of the Cause for beatification of Padre Pio.

1973 January 16: Archbishop Valentino Vailati of Manfredonia submits the documentation to the Congregation for the Causes of the Saints for the *nulla osta* for the introduction of the Cause.

1980 March 3: further documentation submitted by Archbishop Vailati.

1982 November 29: Pope John Paul II signs the decree for the introduction of the process investigating the life and virtues of the Servant of God Padre Pio of Pietrelcina.

1983 March 20: official opening of the process at San Giovanni Rotondo.

1987 May 23: Pope John Paul II prays at the tomb of Padre Pio.

1990 January 21: diocesan process concluded at San Giovanni Rotondo.

December 3: publication of the decree *de validitate* of the process.

1996 December 15: the *Positio* of the process submitted to the Congregation for the Causes of the Saints.

1997 June 13: special Congress of the Congregation gives affirmative vote on the heroic virtues of Padre Pio.

October 21: definitive approval by the Congregation on the heroic virtues of the Servant of God, Padre Pio of Pietrelcina.

December 18: promulgation of the *Decretum super virtutibus* and the conferral on Padre Pio by Pope John Paul II of the title "Venerable."

1998 December 21: the healing of Mrs. Consiglia De Martino of Salerno, the needed miracle for his beatification, is approved by the Congregation for the Causes of Saints and promulgated by Pope John Paul II

1999 May 2: beatification of Padre Pio of Pietrelcina.

2002 June 13: canonization of Padre Pio of Pietrelcina.

SOME SUGGESTED READINGS

Stefano Campanella, *Mercy in Padre Pio,* Staten Island, NY, ST PAULS, 2017.

Charles Mortimer Carty, *Padre Pio: The Stigmatist,* Rockford, IL, TAN Books, 1971 and 1994.

Fabrizio Contessa, *Padre Pio*, Staten Island, NY, ST PAULS/Alba House, 1999.

Jim Gallagher, *Padre Pio: The Pierced Priest*, San Francisco, CA, Harper San Francisco, 1996.

John McCaffery, *Tales of Padre Pio, the Friar of San Giovanni,* Garden City, NY, Doubleday, 1981.

Alessio Parente, *Send me your Guardian Angel: Padre Pio,* Amsterdam, NY, Noteworthy Co., 1983.

Pascal P. Parente, *City on a Mountain: Padre Pio*, Washington, NJ, AMI Pr., 1968.

Bernard Ruffin, *Padre Pio: The True Story,* Huntington, IN, Our Sunday Visitor, 1982 and 1991.

John A. Schug, *Padre Pio: Profile*, Petersham, MA, St. Bede's Publications, 1987.

— and for children —

Eileen Dunn Bertanzette, *Rich in Love: The Story of Padre Pio of Pietrelcina*, Boston, MA, Pauline Books & Media, 1999.

ST PAULS

This book was produced by ST PAULS, the publishing house operated by the Society of St. Paul, an international religious congregation of priests and brothers dedicated to serving the Church through the communications media.

For information regarding this and associated ministries of the Pauline Family of Congregations, write to the Vocation Director:

Vocation Director of the Society of St. Paul
2187 Victory Blvd., Staten Island, NY 10314

Phone us at (718) 865-8844
E-mail: vocation@stpauls.us
www.stpauls.us

That the Word of God be everywhere known and loved.